健康食譜

───附糖尿病・腎臟病食譜
也適用一般減肥者

Healthful Cooking

Recipes for Weight-Watchers and
Patients with Diabetes and/or Renal
Disorders

編輯：財團法人味全文化教育基金會
發行：林麗華
翻譯：嚴　慧
攝影：蕭澤崇

Publisher: Lee Hwa Lin
Editor: Wei-Chuan Cultural
　　　　Educational Foundation
Translator: May Lin
Photographer: T. C. Shiau

序

　　常常有人問起一個問題：「你每天究竟吃了多少卡路里？」因爲我從事於營養學方面的研究，所以大家認爲我對卡路里的概念，一定非常清楚。

　　隨著國民生活水準的提高，近來大衆對於營養問題都很關心，尤其對所謂「現代病」如腦中風、心臟病、糖尿病、高血壓……等等均是攝取過多的卡路里所引起，因此大家對於"卡路里"以及每天所吃的營養素益加重視，而提出此項問題也是無可厚非，總認爲問我即刻會知道吃了多少卡路里，但是事實並非如此。

　　因爲要知道卡路里的含量必須要有量食物的磅秤、食品分析表、計算機等工具方能一一算出，這是很麻煩的事，尤其考慮到每天所吃的食物不同，更是費時，這對於所有研究營養學的人來說，也是一項難題。

　　現代家庭主婦在準備食物的時候，總是很想知道在食物裏究竟含有多少卡路里、蛋白質等 營養成份，尤其糖尿病、腎臟病的患者，如何準備食物，更是一件非常重要的事，家庭主婦在準備吃的同時，若能清楚地知道食物中卡路里及其他營養素的確實含量，則對於一家人之健康管理一定會有莫大的幫助。

　　要達到上述的目的，有一個簡便的方法，首先由營養學專家，撰寫各類食譜，並將其營養素做徹底的分析，詳細列表刊載。這本食譜若能隨時放在身邊使用，在準備食物時，就可參照食譜的記載，調理出適量的菜樣。如此一來，烹煮的食物裏含有多少卡路里、蛋白質、脂肪、維生素等便能一目了然，屈指可數，任何人一天中吃了多少卡路里及其他營養素都可以很輕易地算出來，這不是很方便嗎？

　　長久以來，我就一直想，如有這本食譜，則不但準備食物方便且對於保健方面的貢獻當會更大，適逢味全文化教育基金會出版了有關這方面的食譜，其內容十分適合這方面的需要，可以説是一本非常合乎時代需求的刊物，同時又是彩色印刷，各種食物看起來都秀色可餐，是一本很值得家庭主婦參考的食譜，同時也是一般家庭不可缺少的健康指南，我很眞誠樂意地推薦這本書給大家，希望能藉著這本書使大家在健康上受益無窮。

董大成

●曾任：台大醫學院生化學科教授
　　　　台北醫學院生化學科教授
　　　　台北醫學院院長
　　　　馬偕醫院董事長
　　　　紅十字會台灣省分會會長
●現任：中國食品衛生營養研究基
　　　　金會董事長
　　　　中藥醫學研究基金會董事
　　　　長

Forward

I have often been asked, "Just how many calories do you get in a day?" Having been in the field of nutritional research for many years, I am constantly thought of as knowing precisely how many calories I consume on a daily basis.

As our standards of living improve increasingly, more people are becoming aware of, and are more concerned about nutrition and the problems caused by improper diets. So-called "modern diseases", which include stroke, heart diseases, diabetes and hypertension, are all related to improper eating. People are consequently paying more attention to caloric intake and nutrition in general.

In order to precisely monitor caloric intake on a day to day basis, one would require such tools as, a scale, food analysis table and calculator, to name a few. The process is complicated and time-consuming, and could prove difficult, even for a nutritional specialist.

Many housewives, especially those who have in-house patients suffering from diabeties or kidney disorders, need to be aware of specific contents in each meal prepared. By being well-informed of the caloric and nutritional contents of different foods while preparing meals, the housewife will be better equipped to help prevent the occurrence of modern diseases within her family.

In achieving the above goal, a nutritionist would require detailed analyses of all recipes used. This Cookbook, therefore, has been designed to provide its readers with proper and accurate guidelines in preparing meals for their families. The information given herein will facilitate the calculation of caloric and nutritional values.

I have long wished for this type of book. It not only provides convenience in the preparation of meals, but also contributes greatly towards maintaining optimum health. The Wei-Chuan Cultural Center has finally published such a book, with illustrations that epitomize freshness in each meal prepared. I strongly recommend this book and hope that everyone benefits from its contents!

Ta Cheng Tung

- Experience:
  Professor of Biochemistry, School of Medicine, National Taiwan University
  Professor of Biochemisty, Taipei Medical College
  President of Taipei Medical College
  Chairman of Board of Mackay Memorial Hospital
  President of Taiwan Chapter of the Red Cross Society
- Current Position:
  President of Chinese Food and Nutrition Foundation
  President of the Foundation for Research of Chinese Medicine

專家的話

　　西風東漸，在物質充裕、工作忙碌的生活下，外食機會劇增，正確飲食知識被忽視，慢性病的發生頻率亦隨之上昇，提倡合乎健康之飲食習慣以預防慢性病及輔助治療慢性病乃為當務之急。

　　本食譜即為現代人提供正確之餐點製作方式，尤其針對糖尿病患、腎臟病患等慢性病提供可輔助醫療效果之食譜，希望您能藉此獲得生活的樂趣，享受健康之飲食。

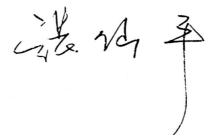

- ●台北醫學院副教授
- ●中華民國營養學會常務理事兼副總幹事
- ●中華民國糖尿病學會理事兼營養委員會召集人
- ●董事基金會常務董事
- ●益富保健療養食品諮詢顧問中心顧問

A Word from a Nutritional Specialist

With the introduction of modern developments, exposure to western concepts, and availability of resources, we now find ourselves engaged in constantly busy work, with more opportunities to dine outside of the home. As a consequence, correct eating habits tend to be neglected, and the frequency of chronic diseases becomes increased. A healthy eating habit is essential in the prevention and control of such chronic disorders.

This Cookbook introduces the correct methods in preparing meals for the modern man, especially for those suffering from Diabetes Mellitus and Chronic Renal Failure. I trust you will find this book enjoyable and helpful in eating towards a healthier you!

Frances C. Ma

- Associate Professor of Taipei Medical College
- Executive Secretary in General and Executive Director of the Nutrition Society located in Taipei China
- Chairman of Nutrition Task Force and Director of the Chinese Diabetes Association
- Executive Director of Tung's Foundation
- Advisor of Enjoy Food Inc.

吃出您的健康來

　　這本 "健康食譜" 從醞釀、策劃到誕生，花了幾近兩年的時間。我們非常慎重地在做這件事情，幾度校正、修改，甚至與專家幾番商議才定稿，所為無它，只希望藉著這本食譜，真能達到我們由衷的期望——吃出每一個人的健康來。

　　時代進步下，多數人不再煩惱自己的營養不足，而變成了營養過剩或營養不均，甚至引起肥胖等文明病，其實這都是吃的不適量、不適當所致。

　　人人會吃，然而要如何「吃出健康」，則是營養學專家近年來致力研究的問題，我們也希望喚醒大家重視食物的價值與補療，因而出版了這本健康食譜，強調「平衡飲食」、「天然食品」、「清淡食品」的重要性。

　　這本健康食譜，除了適用一般減肥者參考外，大致上又可分為三部份。

一、　從第10頁至第59頁是純然的健康食譜。

二、　從第64頁至第93頁是為糖尿病患者製作三十道美味佳餚。

三、　從第96頁至第115頁是腎臟病人的二十道佳餚。

　　除了食譜的配料、作法外，我們詳析每道菜的營養成份及卡路里熱量，讓每個人能知道其之所以屬健康食譜的根本原因。

　　當然，這種製作、設計方法，着實使我們的專任營養師們傷透腦筋，因為唯恐記錄稍有偏失，會影響了它的健康程度。然而，經過兩年的細心琢磨，我們信心十足地推出它，介紹給每一個人，因為它的確是一本——健康食譜。

　　這本書的順利完成與推出，我除了要感謝基金會研究組、家政班、編輯組的通力合作外，也要謝謝董大成教授、張仙平教授提出寶貴的意見及審稿，使這本書更具專業性。

林麗華

Eating Towards A Healthier You

It took us two years from the very beginning of conception through careful planning to the completion of the "Healthful Cooking" Cookbook. It has been finalized as a result of repeated revisions and discussions with experts. We sincerely hope that our readers will find this Cookbook helpful in preparing meals towards achieving optimum health.

With the advancement of time, and progress in living standards, people no longer worry about malnutrition. There is instead, more of a tendency to worry about nutritional imbalance or over-nourishment, as well as over-consumption of fat, all of which are directly related to improper eating habits.

Everyone eats duly, but eating properly to maintain good health has become a problem, which throughout the past years, has been intensively studied by nutritionists. It is with the purpose of reminding you what nourishments are derived from the edibles that this book is compiled, stressing the importance of "Balanced Foods", "Natural Foods" and "Unfatty Foods".

This Cookbook, which is also highly recommended as a general guide to a healthy method of weight-control, is categorized into three sections as follows:
1. Pages 10 through 59, deal with health foods.
2. Pages 64 through 93, recommend 30 delectable dishes for the diabetic.
3. Pages 96 through 115, introduce 20 delicious dishes for those suffering from kidney disorders.

Aside from introducing ingredients and methods of cooking, a concise breakdown of nutrition and calories contained in each dish is listed, thereby explaining to our readers why this has been entitled "Healthful Cooking".

Needless to say, the design and compilation of this book have caused problems for our nutritionists, who are aware that even the slightest error will greatly affect its value. Nevertheless, after two years of careful research, we are finally able to introduce this book to the public with confidence.

We must extend our heartfelt thanks to the Editing, Home Economics and Research Departments of the Fund for their contribution towards the successful completion and publication of this book. In addition, we wish to express our appreciation to Professors T. C. Tuang and S. F. Chang for their valuable suggestions and assistance towards making this book a more professional one.

Elizabeth Hung

目錄 CONTENTS

腎臟病食譜 For Renal Patients

Abbreviation Key:

Original	Weight	Protein	Carbohydrate	Water	Calorie	Sodium	Potassium	Phosphorus
Abbreviation	Wt.	Prot.	CHO	H_2O	Cal	Na	K	P

材料：

小排骨	⋯⋯⋯⋯⋯⋯⋯⋯	400公克
檸檬1個	⋯⋯⋯⋯⋯	榨汁(20公克)
油	⋯⋯⋯⋯⋯⋯⋯⋯⋯	1½大匙
①	水⋯⋯⋯⋯⋯⋯⋯⋯	½杯
	糖、醋⋯⋯⋯⋯⋯⋯	各3大匙
	醬油⋯⋯⋯⋯⋯⋯⋯	1大匙
	太白粉⋯⋯⋯⋯⋯⋯	1小匙

❶排骨洗淨切3公分長段，以①料略醃20分鐘後，將排骨撈起，醃汁留用。

❷鍋熱入油1½大匙，將排骨煎成金黃色，再入剩餘之醃汁，用慢火煮8-10分鐘。

❸起鍋前以大火將汁收乾，再入檸檬汁拌勻即可。

INGREDIENTS:

400g (14 oz)	Pork Ribs
20g (⅔ oz)	Lemon Juice
1½ T.	Cooking Oil
① ½ c.	Water
3 T. each:	Sugar, Vinegar
1 T.	Soysauce
1 t.	Cornstarch

❶ Clean ribs and cut into 3 cm.-long chunks. Marinate with ① for 20 minutes. Remove and retain marinade.

❷ Heat wok; add 1½T. oil, and fry ribs until golden brown. Stir in retained marinade and simmer over low heat for 8 — 10 minutes.

❸ Turn up heat again and allow to boil until liquid has evaporated. Stir in lemon juice, mix well and serve.

項目 Item / 材料 Material	份量，重量（公克）Unit/Wt. (g)	熱量（卡）Energy (Cal.)	蛋白質（公克）Prot. (g)	脂肪（公克）Fat (g)	醣類（公克）CHO (g)
小排骨 Pork Rib	400	1792	53.8	172.8	—
糖 Sugar	3 大匙 T. 45	180	—	—	45
太白粉 Cornstarch	1 小匙 t. 5	16.85	0.06	0.01	4
油 Cooking Oil	1½ 大匙 T. 22.5	198	0	22	0
檸檬汁 Lemon Juice	20	4.8	0.16	0.12	1.2
醋 Vinegar	45	4.95	0.41	—	0.9
合計 Total		2196.6	54.4	195	51.1
一人份 Per Serving		366	9	32.5	8.5

肉捲芹菜　Beef and Celery Rolls

材料：

牛肉薄片⋯⋯⋯ 100公克
芹菜（帶葉）⋯⋯ 150公克
油⋯⋯⋯⋯⋯⋯ 1大匙

① 　醬油⋯⋯⋯⋯⋯¼杯
　糖、酒⋯ 各1小匙
　醋⋯⋯⋯⋯⋯½小匙

② 　高湯⋯⋯⋯⋯⋯ 1杯
　糖、醬油⋯ 各1小匙
　塩⋯⋯⋯⋯⋯⅛小匙

❶芹菜去葉，切5公分長段，川燙30秒，撈起漂涼備用。
❷①料煮沸，入芹菜段，改小火煮約15分鐘盛起。
❸牛肉片攤開，將煮爛之芹菜置於肉片中間，捲成筒狀（圖1）。
❹油一大匙燒熱，將肉捲煎成金黃（圖2），再入②料煮至汁快收乾起鍋即可。

INGREDIENTS:

100g (3½ oz)		Thinly Sliced Beef
150g (5¼ oz)		Celery
1 T.		Cooking Oil
①	¼ c.	Soysauce
	1 t. each:	Sugar, Cooking Wine
	½ t.	Vinegar
②	1 c.	Soup Stock
	1 t. each:	Sugar, Soysauce
	⅛ t.	Salt

❶ Trim off leaves from celery and cut into 5-cm. segments. Scald in boiling water for 30 seconds; remove and allow to cool.

❷ Bring ① to a boil; add celery; simmer over low heat for 15 minutes; remove and set aside.

❸ Spread out beef slices and wrap pre-cooked celery. Roll into cylinders. (Illust. ①).

❹ Heat 1 T. oil in wok or skillet and fry beef rolls until golden brown (Illust. ②). Add ② and simmer until liquid is reduced. Remove and serve.

項目 Item / 材料 Material	份量・重量 Unit/Wt. (公克) (g)		熱量 Energy (卡) (Cal.)	蛋白質 Prot. (公克) (g)	脂肪 Fat (公克) (g)	醣類 CHO (公克) (g)
牛肉 Beef		100	133	18.8	5.8	—
芹菜 Celery		150	15	1.2	0.15	3
油 Cooking Oil	1 大匙 T.	15	180	0	20	0
糖 Sugar	2 小匙 t.	10	40	—	—	10
合　計 Total			368	20	26	13
一人份 Per Serving			61	3.3	4.3	2.2

材料：

小排骨(圖1)······400公克		蕃薯粉········3大匙
桂竹筍(圖1)······300公克		酒··········1小匙
葱段·········10公克	①	蒜末········½小匙
薑片··········2公克		塩、味精、糖、麻油
蒜頭··········8公克		胡椒粉······各⅛小匙
紅辣椒·········4公克		太白粉······½小匙
炸油··········3杯	②	糖·········¼小匙
酒··········1小匙		塩、味精、胡椒粉、
		麻油······各⅛小匙

❶排骨以①料醃10分鐘，「炸油」燒開，將排骨炸成金黃色撈起，桂竹筍撕成粗條(圖2)再切4公分長段川燙撈起，蒜切薄片，紅椒切斜片均備用。

❷鍋中留油1大匙，炒香蒜片，入炸好之排骨、筍絲及酒1小匙，炒勻後盛入碗裡備用。

❸鍋熱，入油½大匙，將葱、薑、紅辣椒及②料略炒後，置排骨上，以大火蒸至爛約30分鐘。即可倒扣於盤中。

■吸油：指排骨過炸之吸油量

INGREDIENTS:

400g (14 oz)	Pork Ribs (Illust. ①)
300g (10½ oz)	Bamboo Shoots (Illust. ①)
10g (⅓ oz)	Green Onion Segments
2g	Sliced Ginger
8g	Garlic Cloves
4g	Hot Red Pepper
3 c.	Cooking Oil (for deep-frying)
1 t.	Cooking Wine

	3 T.	Potato Flour
	1 t.	Cooking Wine
①	½ t.	Minced Garlic
	⅛ t. each:	Salt, Sugar, Sesame Oil, Pepper
	½ t.	Cornstarch
②	¼ t.	Sugar
	⅛ t. each:	Salt, Sesame Oil, Pepper

❶ Rinse pork ribs and marinate with ① for 10 minutes. Heat 3 cups oil in wok and deep fry ribs until golden brown. Remove and drain. Cut bamboo shoots at 4-cm. intervals (Illust. ②), scald in boiling water, remove and drain. Slice garlic cloves and red pepper at a slant; set aside.

❷ Heat wok, add ½ T. oil, and fry sliced garlic until fragrant; add pre-fried ribs and 1 t. wine. Stir-fry, remove and place in a bowl.

❸ Heat wok, add ½ T. oil and quickly stir-fry bamboo shoots, green onion segments, sliced ginger and red pepper together with ②. Remove and place on top of ribs. Steam over high heat until tender (about 30 minutes). Secure serving platter (face-down) on top of bowl, turn over, remove bowl and serve.

材料 Material / 項目 Item	份量，重量 (公克) Unit/Wt. (g)	熱 量 (卡) Energy (Cal.)	蛋白質 (公克) Prot. (g)	脂 肪 (公克) Fat (g)	醣 類 (公克) CHO (g)
小排骨 Pork Ribs	400	1792	53.8	172.8	—
桂竹筍 Bamboo Shoots	300	60	8.7	0.6	9
番薯粉 Potato Flour	3 大匙 T. 45	81	1.62	0.27	18.4
油 Cooking Oil	1½ 大匙 T. 22.5	202.5	0	22.5	0
麻油 Sesame Oil	¼ 小匙 t. 1.25	11.3	0	1.25	0
*吸油 Cooking Oil Absorbed	55	495	0	55	0
合　計 Total		2641.8	64.1	252.42	27.4
一人份 Per Serving		440.3	10.7	42	4.6

材料：

絞豬肉(圖1)……200公克
糙米飯(圖1) ……6大匙
(約75公克)
炸油………………… 4杯

① {
蛋(圖1) ……½個
(約25克)
水、太白粉 各1小匙
酒、塩……各½小匙
味精、麻油各¼小匙
胡椒粉………⅛小匙
}

② {
高湯………… 1杯
糖、醋、番茄醬
………… 各1大匙
醬油、太白粉……
………各½小匙
}

❶絞豬肉放盆子裡攪拌，直到有彈性，再入糙米飯及①
　料拌勻，分成六等份，揉成肉丸(圖2)。
❷炸油燒熱，將肉丸炸至金黃色撈起，放入蒸籠內蒸20
　分鐘，取出排盤。
❸將②料煮開，淋在肉丸上即成。

■吸油：指糙米肉丸過炸之吸油量

INGREDIENTS:

200g (7 oz)　　　　　　　 Ground Pork (Illust. ①)
6 T. (app. 75g/2⅔ oz)　 Cooked Brown Rice (Illust. ①)
4 c.　　　　　　　　　　Cooking Oil (for deep-frying)

① {
½ (app. 25 g)　 Egg (Illust. ①)
1 t. each:　　　 Water, Cornstarch
½ t. each:　　　 Cooking Wine, Salt
¼ t.　　　　　　 Sesame Oil
⅛ t.　　　　　　 Pepper
}

② {
1 c.　　　　　　 Soup Stock
1 T. each:　　　 Sugar, Vinegar, Ketchup
½ t. each:　　　 Soysauce, Cornstarch
}

❶ Stir ground pork in a dish until smooth. Fold in
cooked brown rice, add ① and stir to mix
thoroughly. Divide into 6 portions and roll into
balls. (Illust. ②)

❷ Heat 4 c. oil in a wok and deep-fry meatballs
until golden brown. Remove and place in a dish.
Steam over high heat for 20 minutes. Remove
and arrange on serving platter.

❸ Bring ② to boiling. Sprinkle sauce on meatballs
and serve.

項目 Item 材料 Material	份量，重量 Unit/Wt. (公克)(g)		熱 量 （卡） Energy (Cal.)	蛋白質 （公克） Prot. (g)	脂 肪 （公克） Fat (g)	醣 類 （公克） CHO (g)
絞肉 Ground Pork		200	1098	24.6	109.6	—
糙米飯 Cooked Brown Rice		75	127.5	2.51	0.75	28.28
蛋 Egg		25	43.25	3.13	3.2	0.2
太白粉 Cornstarch	1½ 小匙 t.	7.5	25.3	0.09	0.02	6
番茄醬 Ketchup	1 大匙 T.	15	13.95	0.24	0.05	3.53
糖 Sugar	1 大匙 T.	15	60	—	—	15
＊吸油 Cooking Oil Absorbed		10	90	0	10	0
麻油 Sesame Oil	¼ 小匙 t.	1.25	11.3	0	1.25	0
合 計 Total			1469	30.6	124	53
一人份 Per Serving			245	5.1	21	8.8

材料：

未炸豆包(圖1)…160公克
雞胸肉(去骨、去皮)……
…………… 300公克
四季豆……… 100公克
生香菇……… 120公克
熟紅蘿蔔……… 250公克
葱………… 3枝(30公克)
香菜(圖2)…………6公克
炸油……………… 3杯

① {
酒………… 1小匙
塩、味精……¼小匙
太白粉……… ½小匙
}

② {
水…………… 1杯
醬油………… 2大匙
太白粉……… 1大匙
糖………… ½小匙
塩、味精、麻油…
…………各¼小匙
}

❶雞胸肉切條狀，四季豆切4公分長條，生香菇切條狀，
熟紅蘿蔔切0.5×4公分長段。

❷四季豆、生香菇、紅蘿蔔川燙備用，雞條入①料醃10
分鐘。

❸豆包整張展開，包上雞肉條、四季豆、生香菇、紅蘿
蔔層層捲起，最後用葱綁住，炸油燒6分熱，以中火將
豆包捲炸成金黃色撈起，切成二塊，排盤。

❹②料煮開，淋在豆包捲上，並以香菜撒在中間裝飾即
成。

INGREDIENTS:

160g (5⅔ oz)	Layered Bean Curd Skin (Illust. ①)
300g (10½ oz)	Boned, Skinned Chicken Breast
100g (3½ oz)	String Beans
120g (4¼ oz)	Fresh Black Mushrooms
250g (8¾ oz)	Cooked Carrots
3 stalks (30g/1 oz)	Green Onions
6g	Coriander (Illust. ②)
3 c.	Cooking Oil (for deep-frying)

① {
1 t. — Cooking Wine
¼ t. — Salt
½ t. — Cornstarch
}

② {
1 c. — Water
2 T. — Soysauce
1 T. — Cornstarch
½ t. — Sugar
¼ t. each: — Salt, Sesame Oil
}

❶ Cut chicken breast(s) into thin strips, string beans into 4 cm.-long segments, mushrooms into strips and cooked carrots into 0.5×4 cm. pieces.

❷ In boiling water, scald string beans, mushrooms and carrots. Remove and set aside. Mix chicken with ① and marinate for 10 minutes.

❸ Spread open bean curd skins. Wrap a portion of chicken, string beans, mushrooms and carrots with bean curd skins, and roll into cylinders. Tie each roll with a stalk of green onion. Heat 3 c. oil in wok and over medium heat, gently deep fry rolls until golden brown. Remove, cut into halves and arrange on serving platter.

❹ Bring ② to a boil and sprinkle on rolls. Garnish with coriander prior to serving.

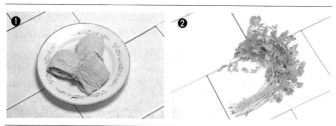

項目 Item 材料 Material	份量・重量 (公克) Unit/Wt. (g)	熱量 (卡) Energy (Cal.)	蛋白質 (公克) Prot. (g)	脂肪 (公克) Fat (g)	醣類 (公克) CHO (g)
未炸豆包 Bean Curd Skin	160	745.6	82.72	40.16	17.92
雞胸肉 Boned Chicken Breast	300	510	94.5	9	0
四季豆 String Beans	100	25	2.8	0.1	3.6
生香菇 Fresh Black Mushrooms	120	25.8	2.61	0.33	11.79
胡蘿蔔 Carrot	250	92.5	2.5	1	20
葱 Green Onion	30	8.1	0.54	0.09	1.68
太白粉 Cornstarch	3½ 小匙 t. 17.5	58.9	0.2	0.05	14
香菜 Coriander	6	+	+	+	+
麻油 Sesame Oil	¼ 小匙 t. 1.25	11.3	0	1.25	0
*吸油 Cooking Oil Absorbed	50	450	0	50	0
合計 Total		1468	185.9	102	69
一人份 Per Serving		245	31	17	11.5

材料：
雞腿3隻‥‥‥約780公克
玻璃紙‥‥‥‥‥‥ 1張

① ｛
黑棗（圖1）‥‥‥6粒
（約6公克）
桂圓（去殼）（圖2）10粒
（約20公克）
芹菜段‥‥‥‥75公克
香菜末‥‥‥‥38公克
葱段‥‥‥‥‥20公克

薑片‥‥‥‥‥‥10公克
紹興酒‥‥‥‥‥ 3大匙
醬油、麻油‥‥‥ 各1小匙
塩、糖‥‥‥‥各½小匙
味精‥‥‥‥‥‥¼小匙
胡椒粉‥‥‥‥‥⅛小匙

❶雞腿切塊及①料，入燉盅醃半小時，以玻璃紙封口入蒸鍋蒸約2小時即可。

INGREDIENTS:

3 (app. 780g/1 lb. 11½ oz.) Chicken Legs

① ｛
6　(app. 6g) Black Dates (Illust. ①)
10 (app. 20g) Shelled Longan (Illust. ②)
75g (2½ oz)　Celery Segments
38g (1¼ oz)　Chopped Coriander
20g (¾ oz)　Green Onion Segments
10g　　　　　Sliced Ginger
3 T.　　　　 Shao Hsing Wine
1 t. each:　　Soysauce, Sesame Oil
½ t.　　　　 Salt
½ t.　　　　 Sugar
⅛ t.　　　　 Pepper

1 sheet　　　Cellophane or Heat-Proof Saran Wrap

❶ Clean chicken legs and chop into bite-size chunks. Place into small casserole, add ① and let stand for ½ hour. Cover with cellophane or saran wrap and secure so that it is air-tight. Steam over high heat for 2 hours.

❶　❷

項目 Item 材料 Material	份量，重量 (公克) Unit/Wt. (g)	熱量 (卡) Energy	蛋白質 (公克) Prot. (g)	脂肪 (公克) Fat (g)	糖類 (公克) CHO (g)
雞腿 Chicken Leg	780	468	78.78	14.82	—
桂圓 Shelled Longan	20	11	0.24	0.04	2.76
黑棗 Black Dates	6	13.92	0.15	0.17	3.6
芹菜 Celery Segments	75	7.5	0.6	0.08	1.5
香菜 Chopped Coriander	38	10.64	1.06	0.19	0.65
葱 Green Onion	20	5.4	0.38	0.06	1.12
薑 Ginger	10	3.7	0.13	0.04	0.77
糖 Sugar	½ 小匙 t. 2.5	10	—	—	2.5
麻油 Sesame Oil	1 小匙 t. 5	45	0	5	0
紹興酒 Shao Hsing Wine	3 大匙 T. 45	151.5	—	—	—
合計 Total		726.7	81.34	20.4	12.9
一人份 Per Serving		121	13.6	3.4	2.2

15

材料：

雞胸肉(去皮)… 120公克
櫻桃蘿蔔片(圖1) 80公克
小酒杯……………… 6個
油………………… ½ 小匙
蛋白……… 3個(90公克)
太白粉…………… ½ 大匙

① ｛ 水………… 2½大匙
　　酒………… ½小匙
　　塩………… ⅛小匙

② ｛ 高湯………… ½杯
　　太白粉…… 1小匙
　　酒………… ½小匙
　　塩………… ¼小匙

❶蛋白打散，雞胸肉剁成泥狀，入①料拌勻後再加蛋白
(邊加邊攪拌)，隨入太白粉拌勻，即爲「雞絨」。

❷小酒杯內均塗油(約½小匙)，放進適量雞絨，用櫻桃
蘿蔔片插成花朵狀(圖2)，水燒開後以小火蒸約3分鐘
，取出排盤。

❸將②料燒滾後，淋在盤上即成。

INGREDIENTS:

120g (4 oz)		Skinned Chicken Breast
80g (2¾ oz)		Sliced Radish (Illust. ①)
6		Miniature Stemless Glasses
½ t.		Cooking Oil
3 (90g/2 oz)		Egg Whites
½ T.		Cornstarch
①	2½ T.	Water
	½ t.	Cooking Wine
	⅛ t.	Salt
②	½ c.	Soup Stock
	1 t.	Cornstarch
	½ t.	Cooking Wine
	¼ t.	Salt

❶ To make batter: Beat egg whites. Chicken is
minced until pasty with smooth consistency. Add
① to minced chicken and mix well. Slowly stir
in egg whites and continue mixing; fold in ½ t.
cornstarch.

❷ Lightly grease glasses with ½ t. oil. Fill glasses
with chicken batter and arrange radish slices
around rims to form florets (Illust. ②). Steam over
low heat for 3 minutes. Detach chicken florets
from glasses and arrange on serving plate.

❸ Bring ② to a boil and pour on florets prior to
serving.

項目 Item 材料 Material	份量，重量 (公克) Unit/Wt. (g)	熱　量 (卡) Energy (Cal.)	蛋白質 (公克) Prot. (g)	脂　肪 (公克) Fat (g)	醣　類 (公克) CHO (g)
鶏胸肉 Skinned Chicken Breast	120	204	37.8	3.6	—
紅蘿蔔 Sliced Carrot	80	29.6	0.8	0.32	6.4
油 Cooking Oil	½ 小匙 t. 2.5	22.5	0	2.5	0
太白粉 Cornstarch	2½ 小匙 t. 12.5	42.1	0.16	0.04	10
蛋白 Egg White	3 個 90	43.2	9.1	0.09	0.72
合　計 Total		341.4	47.9	6.55	17.1
一人份 Per Serving		56.9	8	1.1	2.9

溜 雞 片 Stir-Fried Chicken with Vegetables

材料：

雞胸肉(去皮)(圖1) ……
…………… 300公克
西芹菜(圖1)…… 50公克
豌豆夾 …………… 20公克
木耳 …………… 30公克
葱(切2公分長)6枝60公克
油…………………½杯

① { 水………… 3大匙
太白粉……… 1大匙
塩………… ¼小匙

② { 高湯………… 1杯
酒、太白粉各½大匙
糖………… 1小匙
塩………… ½小匙
味精………… ⅛小匙

❶雞胸肉切薄片，以①料拌匀。豌豆夾折去兩端纖維(圖2)，切兩半。西芹菜切斜段，木耳切粗條均備用。
❷鍋熱入油½杯，將雞片炒熟，見顏色變白即撈起。
❸留油1大匙炒香葱段，入②料燒沸下木耳、豌豆夾、芹菜，再入雞片拌炒均匀即成。
■吸油：指雞片過炒所吸之油量

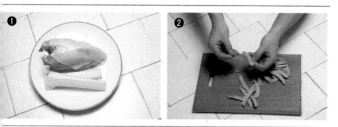

INGREDIENTS:

300g (10½ oz)	Skinned Chicken Breast (Illust. ①)
50g (1¾ oz)	Celery (Illust. ①)
20g (¾ oz)	Snow Pea Pods
30g (1 oz)	Dried Fungus (Black Wood Ear)
60g (2 oz)	Green Onion (2 cm. segments)
½ c.	Cooking Oil

① { 3 T. Water
1 T. Cornstarch
¼ t. Salt

② { 1 c. Soup Stock
½ T. each: Cooking Wine, Cornstarch
1 t. Sugar
½ t. Salt

❶ Cut chicken into thin slices and mix with ①. Trim off veins from both ends of pea pods (Illust. ②) and cut into halves. Cut celery into segments at a slant. Soak wood ear to soften, remove hard stems, and coarsely cut into thick strips. Set aside.
❷ Heat ½ oil in wok and fry sliced chicken until cooked (meat turns pale). Remove and set aside.
❸ Retain 1 T. oil in wok, heat and fry green onion until fragrant. Stir in ② and bring to a boil. Add black wood ear, pea pods and celery. Toss in pre-cooked chicken, mix briskly and serve.

項目 Item / 材料 Material	份量，重量 (公克) Unit/Wt. (g)	熱 量 (卡) Energy (Cal.)	蛋白質 (公克) Prot. (g)	脂 肪 (公克) Fat (g)	醣 類 (公克) CHO (g)
雞胸肉 Skinned Chicken Breast	300	510	94.5	9	—
西芹菜 Celery	50	5	0.4	0.05	1
豌豆夾 Snow Pea Pods	20	6.4	0.2	0.02	1.34
葱 Green Onion	60	16.2	1.08	0.18	3.36
油 Cooking Oil	1 大匙 T. 15	135	0	15	0
太白粉 Cornstarch	1½ 大匙 T. 22.5	75.83	0.28	0.06	18
糖 Sugar	5	20	—	—	5
*吸油 Cooking Oil Absorbed	30	270	0	30	0
合 計 Total		1038	96.5	54	28.7
一人份 Per Serving		173	16	9	4.8

材料：

雞胸肉(去皮)…	450公克	醬油………………	1大匙
小黃瓜…………	48公克	油………………	2大匙
葱………………	2枝	⎧ 醬油…………	1大匙
薑………………	4片	① ⎨ 蒜泥…………	1¼小匙
花椒粉…………	1大匙	⎩ 麻油、醋… 各1小匙

❶ 將雞胸肉洗淨，擦乾水份，以1大匙醬油醃約半小時，再以2大匙熱油煎至金黃色，小黃瓜切3.5公分長段拍碎，排在盤中央備用。

❷ 將煎過之雞肉，以葱、薑、花椒粉抹勻，入電鍋蒸20分鐘，取出待涼(圖1)，餘汁倒出備用，將肉撕成絲狀(圖2)，放於小黃瓜上。

❸ ①料加上蒸肉餘汁拌勻後淋於肉絲上即成。

INGREDIENTS:

	450g (1 lb)	Skinned Chicken Breast
	48g (1½ oz)	Gherkin Cucumbers
	2 stalks	Green Onions
	4 slices	Ginger
	2 T.	Cooking Oil
	1 T.	Peppercorn Powder
	1 T.	Soysauce
	⎧ 1 T.	Soysauce
①	⎨ 1¼ t.	Minced Garlic
	⎩ 1 t. each:	Sesame Oil, Vinegar

❶ Clean chicken breast(s) and pat dry. Marinate in 1 T. soysauce for ½ hour. Heat 2 T. oil and sauté chicken until golden brown. Cut cucumber into 3.5-cm. lengths and smash each section with flat side of cleaver or mallet; place in center of serving platter.

❷ Mix pre-fried chicken with green onions, ginger and peppercorn powder. Steam for 20 minutes; remove and allow to cool (Illust. ①). Strain and retain liquid. Finger-shred chicken (Illust. ②) and place on cucumber.

❸ Mix ① with liquid retained from steamed chicken; sprinkle on shredded chicken and serve.

項目 Item 材料 Material	份量・重量 (公克) Unit/Wt. (g)		熱 量 (卡) Energy (Cal.)	蛋白質 (公克) Prot. (g)	脂 肪 (公克) Fat (g)	醣 類 (公克) CHO (g)
鷄胸 Skinned Chicken Breast		450	765	141.8	13.5	—
小黃瓜 Gherkin Cucumber		48	0.04	0.24	0.05	0.7
油 Cooking Oil	2 大匙 T.	45	405	0	45	0
麻油 Sesame Oil	1 小匙 t.	5	45	0	5	0
合 計 Total			1215	142	63.6	0.7
一人份 Per Serving			203	23.7	10.6	0.1

材料：

嫩鴨半隻	············	650克
油	············	2大匙
檸檬汁	············	1大匙

① 醬油 ············ 2小匙
麻油、酒··· 各1小匙
糖 ············ ½小匙

② 高湯 ············ 1杯
番茄醬 ········ 2大匙
辣醬油 ········ 1大匙
糖 ············ 1½小匙
味精 ············ 1/16小匙

③ 水 ············ 1大匙
太白粉 ········ 1小匙

❶嫩鴨去骨（圖1、2），鴨肉切成二大塊，剔除白筋、黃油（淨肉約270克）以①料醃約半小時備用。

❷鍋熱入油2大匙，將鴨肉煎黃，倒出多餘之油，入②料以小火煮至汁剩約半杯時，即熄火，餘汁倒出備用，鴨肉切成斜片置盤。

❸將剩餘之汁用③料勾成濃芡，入檸檬汁拌勻，淋於鴨肉上即成。

INGREDIENTS:

½ (650g/1 lb. 6¾ oz) Duckling
2 T.　　　　　　　　Cooking Oil
1 T.　　　　　　　　Lemon Juice

① { 2 t.　　　　　Soysauce
1 t. each:　　Sesame Oil, Cooking Wine
½ t.　　　　　Sugar }

② { 1 c.　　　　　Soup Stock
2 T.　　　　　Ketchup
1 T.　　　　　Worcestershire Sauce
1½ t.　　　　Sugar }

③ { 1 T.　　　　　Water
1 t.　　　　　Cornstarch } mix

❶ Remove bones from duckling (Illust. ①, ②) and cut into half. Trim off tendons and fat (net weight approx. 270g/9½ oz.). Mix with ① and marinate ½ hour. Set aside.

❷ Heat wok and add 2 T. oil. Fry duck until meat appears light brown. Drain off excess oil, add ② and simmer over low heat until sauce is reduced to approximately ½ c. Turn off heat, remove duck and retain sauce in wok. Slice duck at an angle and place on serving platter. Reheat remaining sauce and add mixture ③ to thicken. Stir in lemon juice and pour sauce on sliced duck to serve.

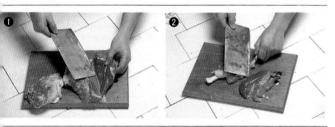

項目 Item 材料 Material	份量，重量 (公克) Unit/Wt. (g)		熱量 (卡) Energy (Cal.)	蛋白質 (公克) Prot. (g)	脂肪 (公克) Fat (g)	醣類 (公克) CHO (g)
鴨肉 Duckling		270	494.1	58.05	27.54	—
油 Cooking Oil	2 大匙 T.	30	270	0	30	0
糖 Sugar	2 小匙 t.	10	40	—	—	10
番茄醬 Ketchup	2 大匙 T.	30	27.9	0.48	0.09	7.05
太白粉 Cornstarch	1 小匙 t.	5	16.85	0.06	0.01	4
麻油 Sesame Oil	1 小匙 t.	5	45	0	5	0
合計 Total			894	58.59	62.64	21.05
一人份 Per Serving			149	9.8	10.44	3.5

材料：

鴨	⋯⋯⋯⋯⋯	半隻(約850公克)
葱	⋯⋯⋯⋯⋯	2枝
薑	⋯⋯⋯⋯⋯	2片
塩	⋯⋯⋯⋯⋯	1½大匙

① {
水⋯⋯⋯⋯⋯ 7杯
酒⋯⋯⋯⋯⋯ 3大匙
醬油⋯⋯⋯⋯⋯ 2大匙
塩、冰糖(圖2)⋯⋯ 各½小匙
花椒、陳皮、小茴香(圖1)⋯⋯
⋯⋯⋯⋯⋯ 各¼小匙
八角(圖2)⋯⋯ 2個(約1公克)
}

❶鴨洗淨，先用開水川燙後，以塩醃約1小時備用。
❷葱、薑及①料煮開，入鴨以小火煮至汁剩約1杯，將汁倒出備用，鴨待涼剁成小塊排盤，食時淋上餘汁即成。

INGREDIENTS:

½ (850g/1 lb. 14 oz.)	Duckling
2 stalks	Green Onions
2 slices	Ginger
1½ T.	Salt

① {
7 c.	Water
3 T.	Cooking Wine
2 T.	Soysauce
½ t. each:	Salt, Rock Sugar (Illust. ②)
¼ t. each:	Dried Orange Peel (Illust. ①),
	Szechuan Peppercorn (Illust. ①),
	Caraway Seeds (Illust. ①)
2 (approx. 1g)	Star Anise (Illust. ②)
}

❶ Rinse duckling; blanch in boiling water; drain and marinate by rubbing exterior and cavity with 1½ T. salt.
❷ In a deep pot, bring ① to a boil with green onion and ginger. Add duckling, reduce heat, cover and simmer over low heat until sauce is reduced to ½ c. Retain sauce. Remove duckling, cut into bite-size pieces and arrange on platter. Prior to serving, sprinkle with retained sauce.
■ If rock sugar is unavailable, plain sugar may be used.

材料\Material	項目 Item	份量，重量(公克) Unit/Wt. (g)	熱量(卡) Energy (Cal.)	蛋白質(公克) Prot. (g)	脂肪(公克) Fat (g)	醣類(公克) CHO (g)
鴨 Duck		850	824.5	96.9	45.9	—
糖 Sugar	½ 小匙 t. 2.5		10	—	—	2.5
酒 Cooking Wine	3 大匙 T. 45		55.5	—	—	—
合計 Total			890	96.9	45.9	2.5
一人份 Per Serving			148	16.2	7.7	0.4

材料：
魩仔魚（圖1）‧‧‧‧‧‧‧‧‧‧‧‧‧‧‧‧‧‧‧‧‧100公克
葱末‧‧‧‧‧‧‧‧‧‧‧‧‧‧‧‧‧‧‧‧‧‧‧‧‧‧‧‧‧‧ 2大匙
油‧‧‧‧‧‧‧‧‧‧‧‧‧‧‧‧‧‧‧‧‧‧‧‧‧‧‧‧‧‧‧‧½大匙

①
低筋麵粉‧‧‧‧‧‧‧‧‧‧‧‧‧‧‧‧‧‧‧‧½杯
水‧‧‧‧‧‧‧‧‧‧‧‧‧‧‧‧‧‧‧‧‧‧‧‧‧‧²⁄₅杯
蛋‧‧‧‧‧‧‧‧‧‧‧‧‧‧‧‧‧‧‧‧½個(25公克)
味精、胡椒粉‧‧‧‧‧‧‧‧‧各⅛小匙

❶魩仔魚川燙1-2秒隨即撈起，瀝乾水份。
❷魩仔魚、葱末及①料調勻備用。
❸鍋熱抹油½大匙(圖2)，倒入上述❷料煎至兩面金黃色
呈薄餅狀即可。

INGREDIENTS:

100g (3½ oz)		Baby Fish (Illust. ①)
2 T.		Minced Green Onion
½ T.		Cooking Oil
①	½ c.	Cake or Pastry Flour
	²⁄₅ c.	Water
	½ (25g/1 oz)	Egg
	⅛ t.	Pepper

❶ Scald baby fish in boiling water for 1-2 seconds. Remove and drain.
❷ Mix baby fish and green onion with ①. Flatten and shape into thin pancake.
❸ Heat frying pan and grease with ½ T. oil (Illust. ②). Gently place pancake in pan and fry until both sides are golden brown. Remove and serve.

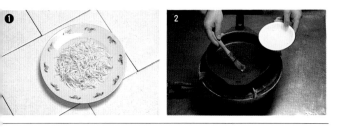

項目 Item　材料 Material	份量，重量 (公克) Unit/Wt. (g)		熱 量 （卡） Energy (Cal.)	蛋白質 (公克) Prot. (g)	脂 肪 (公克) Fat (g)	醣 類 (公克) CHO (g)
魩仔魚 Baby Fish	100		98	20	1.3	0.1
葱 Green Onion	50		13.5	0.9	0.15	2.8
麵粉 Cake or Pastry Flour	½ 杯 C.	75	253.5	8.33	0.9	54.3
蛋 Egg	½ 個 PC.	25	43.25	3.13	3.2	0.2
油 Cooking Oil	½ 大匙 T.	7.5	67.5	0	7.5	0
合 計 Total			476	32.36	13	57.4
一人份 Per Serving			79	5.4	2.1	9.6

21

材料：
草魚(淨肉)······ 300公克
筍片·············50公克
胡蘿蔔片·········50公克
洋菇片···········50公克
玉米筍片·········50公克
葱(3公分)·6段(20公克)
炸油··············· 3杯

① 蛋白············· 1個
太白粉······· 1大匙
酒········· ½大匙
塩········· ½小匙
胡椒粉········· ⅛小匙
葱······1枝(10公克)
薑······2片(5公克)

② 水······· 4大匙
酒······· 1大匙
醬油、麻油 各1小匙
太白粉········· ½小匙
味精········· ¼小匙

❶ 魚肉切3×4×0.5公分塊狀，入①料醃30分鐘備用。
❷ 筍片、胡蘿蔔片、洋菇片、玉米筍片川燙漂涼備用。
❸ 鍋熱入炸油，待溫入魚肉泡油，見顏色變白撈起，留油1大匙爆香葱段再入上述❷料，隨入魚肉及②料拌勻即可。
■ 吸油：指魚片過炸之吸油量

INGREDIENTS:

300g (10½ oz)	Fish Fillets
50g (1¾ oz)	Sliced Bamboo Shoots
50g (1¾ oz)	Sliced Carrots
50g (1¾ oz)	Sliced Mushrooms
50g (1¾ oz)	Sliced Baby Corn
20g (¾ oz)	(6×3cm) Green Onion Segments
3 c.	Cooking Oil (for deep-frying)

①
1	Egg White
1 T.	Cornstarch
½ T.	Cooking Wine
½ t.	Salt
⅛ t.	Pepper
1 stalk (10g)	Green Onion Segments
2 slices (5g)	Ginger

②
4 T.	Water
1 T.	Cooking Wine
1 t. each:	Soysauce, Sesame Oil
½ t.	Cornstarch

項目 Item / 材料 Material	份量，重量 (公克) Unit/Wt. (g)	熱量 (卡) Energy (Cal.)	蛋白質 (公克) Prot. (g)	脂肪 (公克) Fat (g)	醣類 (公克) CHO (g)
草魚 Fish Fillet	300	405	62.1	14.7	1.5
蛋白 Egg White	1 個 PC. 25	12	2.53	0.03	0.2
胡蘿蔔 Sliced Carrot	50	18.5	0.5	0.2	4
玉米筍 Baby Corn	50	80	2.3	0.8	16.05
筍片 Sliced Bamboo Shoot	50	9.5	1.3	0.25	1.2
洋菇 Sliced Mushroom	50	14	1.5	0.15	1.6
葱 Green Onion	35	9.45	0.63	0.11	1.96
油 Cooking Oil	1 大匙 T. 15	135	0	15	0
麻油 Sesame Oil	1 小匙 t. 5	45	0	5	0
*吸油 Cooking Oil Absorbed	20	180	0	20	0
合計 Total		942	76.72	57.2	26.59
一人份 Per Serving		157	12.8	9.5	4.4

❶ Clean and cut fish fillets into 3×4×0.5cm. pieces. Mix in ① and marinate for 30 minutes. Set aside.
❷ Parboil sliced bamboo shoots, carrots, mushrooms and baby corn. Remove and allow to cool.
❸ Heat wok and add 3 c. oil. Immerse fish in oil over medium heat and remove when paled. Retain 1 T. oil in wok, re-heat and fry green onions until fragrant. Add parboiled vegetables from Step ❷; mix in pre-fried fish and ②. Gently stir-fry and serve.

西湖醋魚 West Lake Fish With Vinaigrette Sauce

材料：

魚‥‥‥‥1尾（約600公克）
嫩薑‥‥‥‥‥‥‥‥30公克
胡椒粉‥‥‥‥‥‥‥⅛小匙
油‥‥‥‥‥‥‥‥‥1大匙

① 酒‥‥‥‥‥‥‥‥1小匙
塩‥‥‥‥‥‥‥‥½小匙
胡椒粉‥‥‥‥‥‥⅛小匙
葱‥‥‥‥‥‥‥‥1枝
薑‥‥‥‥‥‥‥‥2片

② 魚湯‥‥‥‥‥‥1½杯
黑醋‥‥‥‥‥‥5大匙
醬油‥‥‥‥‥‥2大匙
糖‥‥‥‥‥‥‥1½大匙
酒‥‥‥‥‥‥‥1大匙
味精‥‥‥‥‥‥½小匙

③ 水‥‥‥‥‥‥‥1½大匙
太白粉‥‥‥‥‥½大匙

❶魚洗淨，從腹部向後剖開，背部不斷（圖1），同時魚骨斬成數段（圖2）以防熱縮。

❷魚以①料醃約15分鐘，入蒸籠以大火蒸約7分鐘。

❸嫩薑切絲泡水，擠乾水份，排在魚身上，並灑上胡椒粉。

❹鍋熱入油1大匙，將②料煮開，再以③料勾芡，而後淋在魚身上即成。

INGREDIENTS:

1 (600g/1 lb. 5 oz)		Fresh Water Fish
30g (1 oz)		Young Ginger
⅛ t.		Pepper
1 T		Cooking Oil
①	1 t.	Cooking Wine
	½ t.	Salt
	⅛ t.	Pepper
	1 stalk	Green Onion Segments
	2 slices	Ginger
②	1½ c.	Fish Broth
	5 T.	Dark Vinegar
	2 T.	Soysauce
	1½ T.	Sugar
	1 T.	Cooking Wine
③	1½ T.	Water } mix
	½ T.	Cornstarch

❶ Scale and clean fish. Split lengthwise through belly, Do not cut through back (Illust. ①). Chop large bones at intervals (Illust. ②) to prevent shrinkage while cooking.

❷ Marinate fish with ① for 15 minutes. Place on platter and steam over high heat for 7 minutes.

❸ Shred young ginger into thin strips and soak in water for a few minutes. Squeeze out excess water from shredded ginger and lay on top of steamed fish. Sprinkle fish with ⅛ t. pepper.

❹ Heat wok and add 1 T. oil. Pour in ② to make sauce, bring to a boil and thicken with mixture ③. Pour over fish and serve immediately.

項目 Item / 材料 Material	份量，重量（公克）Unit/Wt. (g)	熱量（卡）Energy (Cal.)	蛋白質（公克）Prot. (g)	脂肪（公克）Fat (g)	醣類（公克）CHO (g)
魚 Fresh Water Fish	600	504	76.8	18	1.8
油 Cooking Oil	1 大匙 T 15	135	0	15	0
糖 Sugar	1½ 大匙 T. 22	88	—	—	22
嫩薑 Young Ginger	40	14.8	0.52	0.16	3.08
太白粉 Cornstarch	½ 大匙 T. 7.5	25.3	0.09	0.02	6
合計 Total		767	77.4	33.18	32.9
一人份 Per Serving		128	13	5.5	5.5

材料：

鯧魚肉	230公克	
豆皮	3張	
葱段	4枝	
薑片	4片	
葱、薑、蒜末	各1小匙	
油	5杯	

① 蛋白……½個
酒、太白粉 各1小匙
塩……½小匙
味精……¼小匙
胡椒粉……⅛小匙

② 水、麵粉… 各1大匙
水……½杯

③ 糖、醋、番茄醬 各2大匙
醬油……1小匙
麻油……¼小匙

④ 水……1大匙
太白粉……½大匙

❶ 鯧魚肉洗淨，切成12份，用葱、薑與①料拌勻，醃約20分鐘

❷ 豆皮每張切成4小張(圖1)共12小張，將魚肉包好成ㄘ型，並用調好之②料糊好缺口(圖2)。

❸ 鍋熱入油5杯，將包好的魚塊下鍋炸至外表呈金黃色撈起，瀝乾排盤。

❹ 鍋熱入油1大匙，爆香葱、薑、蒜末後入③料煮開，起鍋前用④料勾芡，將汁淋在豆皮包魚上面即成。

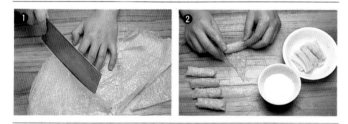

INGREDIENTS:

230g (8 oz)	Pomfret Fillets
3 sheets	Bean Curd Skin
4 segments	Green Onion
4 slices	Ginger
1 t. each:	Minced Green Onion, Minced Ginger, Minced Garlic
5 c.	Cooking Oil (for deep-frying)

① ½ — Egg White
1 t. each: — Cooking Wine, Cornstarch
½ t. — Salt
⅛ t. — Pepper

② 1 T. — Water } mix
1 T. — Flour

③ ½ c. — Water
2 T. each: — Sugar, Vinegar, Ketchup
1 t. — Soysauce
¼ t. — Sesame Oil

④ 1 T. — Water } mix
½ T. — Cornstarch

❶ Clean fish fillets and cut into 12 pieces. Mix with green onion segments, ginger slices and ① Marinate for 20 minutes.

❷ Cut each bean curd skin into 4 sheets (Illust. ①) (total 12 sheets). Place a piece of fish on each sheet of bean curd skin and wrap into squares. Seal openings with ② (Illust. ②).

❸ Heat wok and add 5 c. oil. Deep-fry wrapped fish until outer layer appears golden brown. Remove, drain and arrange on serving plate.

❹ Leave 1 T. oil in wok and fry minced green onion, ginger and garlic until fragrant. Stir in ③ and bring to a boil. Thicken sauce by adding mixture ④. Stir and sprinkle sauce on wrapped fish.

項目 Item 材料 Material	份量，重量 Unit/Wt. (g)		熱量 Energy (Cal.)	蛋白質 Prot. (g)	脂肪 Fat (g)	醣類 CHO (g)
鯧魚肉 Pomfret Fillet		230	170.2	37.72	0.69	0.69
豆皮 Bean Curd Skin		20	93.2	10.34	5.02	2.24
蛋白 Egg White	½ 個 PC.	15	7.2	15.2	0.15	1.2
太白粉 Cornstarch	2½ 小匙 t.	12.5	42.1	1.6	0.4	10
麵粉 Flour	1 大匙 T.	15	50.93	1.55	0.2	10.95
糖 Sugar	2 大匙 T.	30	120	—	—	30
番茄醬 Ketchup	2 大匙 T.	30	27.9	0.48	0.09	7.05
麻油 Sesame Oil	¼ 小匙 t.	1.25	11.3	0	1.25	0
油 Cooking Oil	1 大匙 T.	15	135	0	15	0
*吸油 Cooking Oil Absorbed			720	0	80	0
合計 Total			1378	66.9	103	62.1
一人份 Per Serving			229	11.1	17	10.4

材料：

魩仔魚(圖1)⋯⋯110公克	
小黃瓜⋯⋯⋯⋯ 100公克	
榨菜末(圖2) ⋯⋯1大匙	
(約12公克)	
白芝麻(圖2)⋯⋯⋯1大匙	

① 醋⋯⋯⋯⋯⋯ 4大匙
糖⋯⋯⋯ 1⅔大匙
麻油⋯⋯⋯⋯½小匙
塩⋯⋯⋯⋯⋯¼小匙

❶魩仔魚入滾水中川燙1-2秒，隨即撈起瀝乾水份。
❷小黃瓜切薄片，撒塩少許，待軟洗淨後拭乾。
❸鍋熱入白芝麻以小火乾炒，炒至香味溢出。
❹將魩仔魚、榨菜末、小黃瓜片及①料拌勻放於盤內，
　洒上白芝麻即成。

INGREDIENTS:

110g (3¾ oz)	Baby Fish (Illust. ①)
100g (3½ oz)	Gherkin Cucumbers
1 T. (12g/½ oz)	Minced Szechuan Pickled Mustard Greens (Illust. ②)
1 T.	White Sesame Seeds (Illust. ②)

①
4 T.	Vinegar
1⅔ T.	Sugar
½ t.	Sesame Oil
¼ t.	Salt

❶ Blanch baby fish in boiling water for 1-2 seconds. Remove and drain.
❷ Cut gherkin cucumbers into thin slices. Mix with a dash of salt. When softened, rinse thoroughly and pat dry.
❸ In a dry, heated pan, parch sesame seeds by stirring until fragrant.
❹ Toss baby fish, minced pickled mustard greens and sliced cucumbers with ① and place on serving platter. Sprinkle sesame seeds on top and serve.

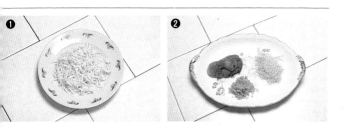

材料\Material	項目 Item　份量，重量 (公克) Unit/Wt. (g)	熱　量 (卡) Energy (Cal.)	蛋白質 (公克) Prot. (g)	脂　肪 (公克) Fat (g)	醣　類 (公克) CHO (g)
魩仔魚 Baby Fish	110	107.8	22	1.43	0.11
小黃瓜 Gherkin Cucumber	100	8	0.5	0.1	1.6
白芝麻 White Sesame Seeds	15	87.9	2.42	8.37	2.34
糖 Sugar	1⅔ 大匙 T. 25	100	—	—	25
麻油 Sesame Oil	½ 小匙 t. 2.5	22.5	0	2.5	0
合　計 Total		326	24.9	12.4	29.1
一人份 Per Serving		54.4	4.2	2	4.9

材料：

牛肉	225公克
青椒	225公克
葱	1枝
薑	3片
油	4大匙

① { 水 …… 2大匙 / 醬油露、太白粉 …… 各1½小匙 / 酒 …… 1小匙 / 塩 …… ¼小匙

② { 水 …… 2大匙 / 糖 …… ¾小匙 / 塩、味精 …… 各⅛小匙

❶牛肉切細絲，以①料醃半小時，青椒去籽切細絲。

❷醃好的牛肉絲拌入1大匙油，鍋熱入油2大匙，以大火炒至肉變白即可起鍋。

❸鍋熱入油1大匙爆香葱、薑，隨入青椒及②料炒熟後，再放入牛肉絲一起拌勻即成。

INGREDIENTS:

225g (8 oz)	Beef
225g (8 oz)	Green Bell Peppers
1 stalk	Green Onion Segments
3 slices	Ginger
4 T.	Cooking Oil

① { 2 T. — Water / 1½ t. each: — Soysauce, Cornstarch / 1 t. — Cooking Wine / ¼ t. — Salt

② { 2 T. — Water / ¾ t. — Sugar / ⅛ t. — Salt

❶ Shred beef into thin strips and marinate with ① for ½ hour. Wash green peppers, remove seeds and cut into thin strips.

❷ Add 1 T. oil to marinated beef and mix well. Heat wok, add 2 T. oil and stir-fry beef over high heat until beef is paled. Remove and set aside.

❸ Heat wok, add 1 T. oil and stir-fry green onion and ginger until fragrant. Then add green pepper and ②. Stir until cooked. Add pre-fried beef, mix well and serve.

項目 Item / 材料 Material	份量，重量 (公克) Unit/Wt. (g)	熱量 (卡) Energy (Cal.)	蛋白質 (公克) Prot. (g)	脂肪 (公克) Fat (g)	醣類 (公克) CHO (g)
牛肉 Beef	225	299	42.3	13.05	—
青椒 Green Bell Pepper	225	36	2.25	0.45	7.43
油 Cooking Oil	3 大匙 T. 45	405	0	45	0
太白粉 Cornstarch	1½ 小匙 t. 7.5	25.3	0.09	0.02	6
糖 Sugar	¾ 小匙 t. 3.75	15	—	—	3.75
合計 Total		780	44.6	58.5	17.2
一人份 Per Serving		130	7.4	9.8	2.9

生炒牛肉鬆 Minced Beef

材料：

絞瘦牛肉………	225公克	
米粉……………	5公克	
洋葱末…………	150公克	
炸油……………	6杯	

① 洋菇末………75公克
胡蘿蔔末……75公克
荸薺末………75公克
芹菜末………37公克

② 醬油露……1½大匙
塩…………⅛小匙
蛋黃…………1個

③ 酒…………½大匙
麻油、醬油露………
各1小匙
胡椒粉………¼小匙

❶ 絞牛肉以②料醃約半小時，米粉以熱油炸鬆（圖1），見膨脹即撈起，瀝乾盛盤。
❷ 鍋熱入油1大匙，將醃好之絞牛肉炒熟備用。
❸ 鍋熱入油1大匙炒香洋葱，再入①料同炒，隨即加入③料及牛肉拌勻即可放在炸好之米粉上。
■ 此道菜可以生菜捲（圖2）或夾麵包方式食之
■ 吸油：指米粉過炸所吸油量

INGREDIENTS:

225g (8 oz)		Ground Lean Beef
5g (⅙ oz)		Rice Noodles
150g (5¼ oz)		Minced Onion
6 c.		Cooking Oil (for deep-frying)
①	75g (2½ oz)	Minced Button Mushrooms
	75g (2½ oz)	Minced Carrots
	75g (2½ oz)	Minced Water Chestnuts
	37g (1¼ oz)	Minced Celery
②	1½ T.	Soysauce
	⅛ t.	Salt
	1	Egg Yolk
③	½ T.	Cooking Wine
	1 t. each:	Sesame Oil, Soysauce
	¼ t.	Pepper

❶ Mix ground beef with ② and marinate for ½ hour. Deep-fry rice noodles in hot oil until loose and expanded (Illust. ①); remove, drain and place on serving plate.
❷ Heat wok and add 1 T. oil. Stir-fry marinated beef until cooked; remove and drain.
❸ Re-heat wok, add 1 T. oil and stir-fry minced onions until slightly browned and fragrant. Add minced vegetables (①) and fry briskly. Stir in ③ and pre-fried beef. Mix thoroughly and pour over fried rice noodles.
■ May be served with lettuce leaves to wrap minced beef mixture (Illust. ②).

材料 Material	項目 Item 份量，重量 （公克） Unit/Wt. (g)	熱 量 （卡） Energy (Cal.)	蛋白質 （公克） Prot. (g)	脂 肪 （公克） Fat (g)	醣 類 （公克） CHO (g)
絞瘦牛肉 Ground Leen Beef	225	299	42.3	13.05	—
洋葱 Minced Onion	150	37.5	1.35	0.6	7.5
洋菇 Minced Button Mushroom	75	12	2.25	0.38	2.7
胡蘿蔔 Minced Carrot	75	27.8	0.75	0.3	6
荸薺 Minced Water Chestnut	75	48	0.83	0.08	11.7
芹菜 Minced Celery	37	3.7	0.30	0.04	0.74
蛋黃 Egg Yolk	20	69.6	2.96	6.22	0.18
乾米粉 Rice Noodle	5	12.7	0.13	0.01	2.93
麻油 Sesame Oil	5	315	0	35	0
油 Cooking Oil	2 大匙 T. 30	270	0	30	0
*吸油 Cooking Oil Absorbed	7	63	0	7	0
合 計 Total		1158	50.9	93	31.8
一人份 Per Serving		193	8.5	15.5	5.3

材料：

牛肉	150公克	
蛋白	3個(90公克)	
水	3大匙	
①	水	1大匙
	醬油、太白粉	
	各½大匙	
	酒	1小匙

② 香菜 4大匙
葱花 2大匙
胡椒粉、麻油 各⅛小匙

③ 高湯 6杯
塩 1½小匙
味精 ⅛小匙

④ 水 5大匙
太白粉 4大匙

❶牛肉切片以①料醃20分鐘，蛋白加水打勻，②料置入碗內備用(圖1)。

❷③料燒開，將牛肉片一片一片放入湯內，煮沸後再以④料勾芡，淋上蛋白液，並攪動使其散開，立即熄火，倒在備好之湯碗內(圖2)即成。

INGREDIENTS:

150g (5¼ oz)		Beef
3 (90g/3 oz)		Egg Whites
3 T.		Water
①	1 T.	Water
	½ T. each:	Soysauce, Cornstarch
	1 t.	Cooking Wine
②	4 t.	Coriander
	2 T.	Chopped Green Onions
	⅛ t. each:	Pepper, Sesame Oil
③	6 c.	Soup Stock
	1½ t.	Salt
④	5 T.	Water
	4 T.	Cornstarch } mix

❶ Cut beef into thin slices and marinate with ① for 20 minutes. Mix egg whites with 3 T. water and beat until thoroughly blended. Place all of ② (clean coriander sprigs) in large serving bowl (Illust. ①).

❷ Bring ③ to a boil and drop beef slices one by one. Allow to boil again, and thicken by stirring in ④. Gradually pour in eggwhite/water mixture and stir gently until separated. Extinguish heat and immediately pour into serving bowl over ② and serve (Illust. ②).

材料 Material	項目 Item 份量 • 重量 (公克) Unit/Wt. (g)	熱量 (卡) Energy (Cal.)	蛋白質 (公克) Prot. (g)	脂肪 (公克) Fat (g)	醣類 (公克) CHO (g)
牛肉 Beef	150	199.5	28.2	8.7	—
蛋白 Egg White	3個 PC. 90	43.2	9.01	0.09	0.72
葱 Green Onion	20	5.4	0.36	0.06	1.12
香菜 Coriander	20	5.6	0.56	0.1	0.34
太白粉 Cornstarch	4½ 大匙 T. 67.5	225.79	0.84	0.17	53.6
油 Cooking Oil	⅛ 小匙 t. 0.625	5.6	—	0.625	—
合 計 Total		485	39.05	9.7	55.78
一人份 Per Serving		81	6.5	1.6	9.3

五香牛肉　Five-Spiced Beef

材料：
牛腱(圖1)‥‥‥‥‥‥2個(約1350公克)
糖‥‥‥‥‥‥‥‥‥‥‥‥‥‥ 4大匙
麻油‥‥‥‥‥‥‥‥‥‥‥ 1½大匙
①
水‥‥‥‥‥‥‥‥‥‥‥‥‥‥ 8杯
醬油‥‥‥‥‥‥‥‥‥‥‥‥‥ ¾杯
酒‥‥‥‥‥‥‥‥‥‥‥‥‥ 1大匙
八角(圖2)‥‥‥‥‥‥‥‥‥‥‥1顆

❶牛腱川燙，撈出洗淨，放入鍋內，並入①料，燒開後
，改小火煮約2小時至筷子可將肉插透時，加糖續煮10
分鐘，呈濃稠狀，再加麻油1大匙即熄火，撈出。待冷
切片，淋上麻油½大匙即成。
■燒好之牛肉，可置冰箱內保存三天，隨時取出切片食
之。

INGREDIENTS:

2 (1,350g/3 lbs)		Beef Shanks (Illust. ①)
4 T.		Sugar
1½ T.		Sesame Oil
①	8 c.	Water
	¾ c.	Soysauce
	1 T.	Cooking Wine
	1	Star Anise (Illust. ②)

❶ Blanch whole beef pieces in boiling water.
Remove and clean by rinsing. Place into deep
stewing pot, add ① and bring to boiling. Reduce
heat and simmer for 2 hours (or until beef is soft
enough to be poked through with chopstick).
Add 4 T. sugar and continue simmering for 10
more minutes. Remove and allow to cool. To
serve, slice and sprinkle with ½ T. sesame oil.
■ May be kept in refrigerator for up to 3 days and
served as cold-cuts.

❶　❷

材料 Material / 項目 Item	份量・重量 (公克) Unit/Wt. (g)	熱量 (卡) Energy (Cal.)	蛋白質 (公克) Prot. (g)	脂肪 (公克) Fat (g)	醣類 (公克) CHO (g)
牛腱 Beef Shank	1350	1796	253.8	78.3	—
糖 Sugar	4 大匙 T. 60	240	—	—	60
油 Cooking Oil	1½ 大匙 T. 22.5	203	—	22.5	—
合計 Total		2239	253.8	100.8	60
一人份 Per Serving		373	42.3	16.8	10

牛肉粉絲　Beef with Vermicelli

材料：

牛肋條(圖1)……900公克
糖………………1大匙
粉絲(圖2)¼把(約7公克)

①　水……………8杯
醬油…………3大匙
酒…………1½大匙
葱段…………4段
薑片…………2片

❶牛肋條整塊川燙撈起，入快鍋內加①料同煮，先以大火燒滾，再以小火煮約1小時至牛肋條熟透後，再加糖1大匙續煮10分鐘，即熄火撈出待涼切片,牛肉湯汁備用。

❷粉絲以開水泡軟撈出沖冷水備用。

❸備中碗1個，將牛肋條片整齊排列于碗底，再舖上粉絲，淋上½杯的牛肉湯汁，蒸3分鐘時倒扣在盤中即成。

■使用快鍋方法：快鍋須待涼方可打開。

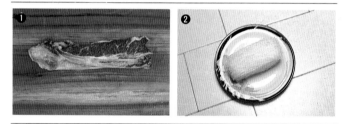

INGREDIENTS:

900g (2 lbs)	Beef Ribs (Illust. ①)
1 T.	Sugar
¼ bunch (7g/¼ oz)	Bean Threads (Illust. ②)

①	8 c.	Water
	3 T.	Soysauce
	1½ T.	Cooking Wine
	4 segments	Green Onion
	2 slices	Ginger

❶ Blanch whole chunk(s) of beef in boiling water. Remove and place in pressure cooker with ①. Bring to boiling, reduce heat and cook for 1 hour. (Beef should be tender enough to be poked through with chopstick.) Add 1 T. sugar and continue cooking for 10 minutes. Turn off heat, remove and allow to cool. Slice beef, retain sauce and set aside.

❷ Soak bean threads until soft. Rinse with cold water and set aside.

❸ In a medium-sized bowl, arrange beef slices on bottom layer. Place pre-soaked bean threads on top of beef. Pour retained beef sauce on top and allow to soak for 3 minutes. To serve, invert bowl onto platter.

項目 Item 材料 Material	份量·重量 (公克) Unit/Wt. (g)	熱量 (卡) Energy (Cal.)	蛋白質 (公克) Prot. (g)	脂肪 (公克) Fat (g)	醣類 (公克) CHO (g)
牛肋條 Beef Ribs	900	2385	150.3	193.5	—
粉絲 Bean Threads	10	28	—	—	7
糖 Sugar	1 大匙 T　15	60	—	—	15
合計 Total		2473	150.3	193.5	22
一人份 Per Serving		412	25.1	32.3	3.7

別有洞天　Stuffed Beancurd Pockets

材料：

方型油豆腐皮‥‥‥‥6個
（60公克）
干瓢‥‥‥‥‥‥‥‥20公克
蛋‥‥‥‥6個（約300公克）

① 高湯‥‥‥‥‥ 2½杯
酒‥‥‥‥‥ 1½大匙
醬油‥‥‥‥ 1大匙
糖‥‥‥‥‥ 2小匙
塩‥‥‥‥‥ ½小匙
味精‥‥‥‥ ⅛小匙

❶水燒開，入油豆腐皮川燙撈起，擠乾水份，干瓢入滾
　水中煮軟，撈起漂涼擠乾水份後，切6公分長段均備用
❷將油豆腐皮一邊剪開，蛋打在小碗內（不可打散），再
　將一個蛋倒進一個油豆腐皮內（圖1），封口以干瓢綁緊
　（圖2）。
❸①料燒開，將包好的油豆腐包放入排好，加蓋以中火
　煮15分鐘取出，拆下干瓢，將油豆腐包切開置盤上。

INGREDIENTS:

6 (60g/2 oz)	Fried Bean Curd Squares
20g (¾ oz)	Dried Gourd Strips
6 (300g/10½ oz)	Eggs

①
2½ c.	Soup Stock
1½ T.	Cooking Wine
1 T.	Soysauce
2 t.	Sugar
½ t.	Salt

❶ Quickly scald bean curd squares in boiling water.
Remove and squeeze out excess water. Boil gourd
strips until soft; remove and allow to cool; cut
into 6 cm. segments and set aside.

❷ Cut open 1 side of each bean curd square.
Break 6 eggs into a small bowl (do not beat).
Slide 1 egg into each bean curd pocket (Illust.
①). Close pockets by tying securely with gourd
strips (Illust. ②).

❸ Bring ① to a boil. Add stuffed bean curd pockets,
cover and cook over medium heat for 15 minutes.
Remove gourd strips from pocket openings. Cut
into halves and serve.

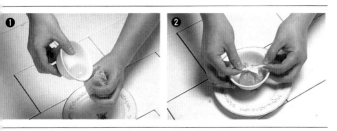

材料 Material	項目 Item 份量，重量 （公克） Unit/Wt. (g)		熱量 （卡） Energy (Cal.)	蛋白質 （公克） Prot. (g)	脂肪 （公克） Fat (g)	醣類 （公克） CHO (g)
油豆腐皮 Fried Bean Curd Square	6 個 PC.	60	150.6	12.3	12.24	1.32
蛋 Egg	6 個 PC.	300	462	33.3	34.2	2.1
糖 Sugar	2 小匙 t.	10	40	—	—	10
干瓢 Dried Gourd Strips		20	39.6	1.36	0.12	9.86
合計 Total			692	47	46.6	23.3
一人份 Per Serving			115	7.8	7.8	3.9

四味蛋包肉 Four-Flavored Pork Egg Rolls

6人份
serves

材料：

里肌肉(切絲)…… 225公克
韭黄(切段)……… 150公克
木耳(切絲)………75公克
蛋………4個(約200公克)
油………………2杯

① { 蛋……半個(約25公克)
醬油、太白粉 各1小匙
味精…………¼小匙
胡椒粉、塩 各⅛小匙

② { 水………1½小匙
太白粉………1小匙

③ { 醬油露………2大匙
水、芥茉粉 各1大匙

④ { 甜麵醬………1½大匙
醬油、麻油 各1大匙
糖…………¾大匙
味精…………½小匙

⑤ { 醬油………3大匙
芝麻醬、辣醬油
………各2大匙
鎮江醋………1大匙
麻油、糖 各2小匙
花椒粉………1小匙
薑末…1大匙(7公克)
葱末…1大匙(6公克)
蒜末…1大匙(5公克)

⑥ { 番茄醬………2大匙

❶肉絲①料略醃，鍋熱入油2杯，以温油將肉絲泡熟，撈出瀝乾備用。

❷鍋熱入油1大匙，炒香韭黄、木耳，再入肉絲，以②料勾芡拌勻起鍋即成餡。分成六份備用。

❸鍋熱抹少許油(約1大匙)，入蛋液煎成蛋皮(4個蛋約煎成6個蛋皮)取出待涼，再把餡置蛋皮中間，包成長方形(圖1)。

❹鍋熱入油1大匙，將包好之蛋捲煎成兩面金黃色盛起。

❺食時，將蛋皮捲切開，再依各人喜好沾3 4 5 6，4種沾料(圖2)即成。

INGREDIENTS:

225g (8 oz)	Shredded Pork Tenderloin
150g (5⅓ oz)	Yellow Chinese Chive Segments
75g (2⅔ oz)	Pre-Soaked and Shredded Black Wood Ea
4 (200g/7¾ oz)	Eggs
2 c.	Cooking Oil

① { ½ (25g) Egg
1 t. each: Soysauce, Cornstarch
⅛ t. each: Pepper, Salt

② { 1½ t. Water
1 t. Cornstarch } mix

③ { 2 T. Soysauce
1 T. each: Water Dry Mustard } mixod

④ { 1½ T. Sweet Bean Paste
1 t. each: Soysauce, Sesame Oil } mix
¾ T. Sugar

⑤ { 3 T. Soysauce
2 T. each: Sesame Paste,
Worcestershire Sauce
1 t. each: Dark Vinegar,
(7g) Minced Ginger,
(6g) Minced Green Onion,
(5g) Minced Garlic Cloves } mix
2 t. each: Sesame Oil, Sugar
1 t. Peppercorn Powder

⑥ { 2 T. Ketchup

❶ Add ① to shredded pork and mix thoroughly. Hea wok and add 2 c. oil. Soak shredded pork in lukewarn oil until done, remove and drain. Retain oil.

❷ Re-heat wok, add 1 T. oil and stir-fry chives with shredded wood ear until fragrant. Add pre-cooked pork, followed by mixture ② to thicken. Stir, remove and divide into 6 portions. This is the filling.

❸ To make 6 egg sheets: Beat 4 eggs. Heat wok and lightly grease it. Pour in a portion of the egg batter and gently swirl wok to form a thin crepe-like sheet. When firm carefully lift the edge and turn over. Remove and repea until all 6 are made. Allow to cool. Spread a portion o the filling on each egg sheet and wrap into rectangles (Illust ①).

❹ Re-heat wok and add 1 T. oil Gently fry both sides o stuffed egg sheets until golden brown. Remove.

❺ Cut open stuffed egg sheets and place on platter. Serve with pre-mixed sauces ③, ④, ⑤ and ⑥. (Illust. ②).

材料 Material	項目 Item	份量、重量 (公克) Unit/Wt. (g)	熱 量 (卡) Energy (Cal.)	蛋白質 (公克) Prot. (g)	脂 肪 (公克) Fat (g)	醣 類 (公克) CHO (g)
里肌肉 Shredded Pork Tenderloin		225	781	32.9	71.1	—
蛋 Egg	5½ 個 PC.	225	389	28.1	28.8	1.8
韭黄 Yellow Chinese Chives		150	22.5	2.85	0.6	2.7
木耳 Pre-Soaked and Shredded Black Wood Ear		75	85	7.58	0.9	49
油 Cooking Oil	2 大匙 T.	30	270	—	30	
合 計 Total			1548	71.43	131.4	53.5
一人份 Per Serving			258	11.9	21.9	8.9

材料：

黃豆	150公克
蛋	3個(150公克)
葱花	1大匙
油	2大匙
①{ 塩	½小匙
味精	⅛小匙

❶黃豆洗淨泡水一夜，再用水煮軟到熟，瀝乾，蛋打散均勻備用。

❷鍋熱入油2大匙，倒入蛋液，炒至半熟，入黃豆略炒，再入①料拌炒均勻，起鍋前撒上葱花即成。

INGREDIENTS:

150g (5¼ oz)	Soy Beans
3 (150g/5⅗ oz)	Eggs
2 T.	Cooking Oil
1 T.	Chopped Green Onions
① ½ t.	Salt

❶ Wash soy beans and soak in water overnight. Boil until thoroughly cooked. Remove and drain. Beat eggs and set aside.

❷ Heat wok and add 2 T. oil. Pour in egg batter and stir-fry until half-done. Immediately add soy beans and stir. Season with ① and mix. Sprinkle chopped green onions on omelette and serve.

項目 Item 材料 Material	份量，重量 （公克） Unit/Wt. (g)	熱量 （卡） Energy (Cal.)	蛋白質 （公克） Prot. (g)	脂肪 （公克） Fat (g)	醣類 （公克） CHO (g)
黃豆 Soy Bean	150	488	55.2	27.2	41.55
蛋 Egg	3 個 PC. 150	260	18.8	19.2	0.91
油 Cooking Oil	2 大匙 T. 30	270	—	30	—
合計 Total		1018	74	76.4	42.5
一人份 Per Serving		170	12.3	12.7	7.1

蝦仁燒豆腐 Shrimps with Bean Curd

材料：

蝦仁……………30公克
豆腐……3塊（300公克）
熟豌豆仁………2大匙
（約30公克）
油………………2大匙
① { 塩、酒、太白粉……
　　……………各⅟₁₆小匙

② { 高湯……………1杯
　　醬油…………1大匙
　　太白粉………½大匙
　　酒、糖……各½小匙
　　塩……………¼小匙
　　味精…………⅛小匙

❶蝦仁去腸泥（圖1）洗淨 以①料略醃，入滾水中燙熟撈出備用。
❷豆腐吸乾水份後切塊備用。
❸鍋熱入油2大匙，以大火將豆腐塊煎至表面呈金黃色（圖2），入②料，燒開後續入蝦仁及豌豆仁拌炒均勻即可盛盤。

INGREDIENTS:

30g (1 oz)		Raw Shelled Shrimp
3 (300g/10½ oz)		Bean Curd Squares
2 T. (30g/1 oz)		Cooked Snow Peas
①	2 T.	Cooking Oil
	⅟₁₆ t. each:	Salt, Cooking Wine, Cornstarch
②	1 c.	Soup Stock
	1 T.	Soysauce
	½ T.	Cornstarch
	½ t. each:	Cooking Wine, Sugar
	¼ t.	Salt

❶ Clean and devein shrimp (Illust. ①); mix with ① blanch in boiling water, remove and drain. Se aside.
❷ Rinse bean curd squares, pat dry and dice. Se aside.
❸ Heat wok, add 2 T. oil and fry bean curd ove high heat until golden brown (Illust ②). Add (and bring to a boil; add shrimp and snow pea Mix and serve.

材料 Material	項目 Item 份量，重量 (公克) Unit/Wt. (g)		熱量 (卡) Energy (Cal.)	蛋白質 (公克) Prot. (g)	脂肪 (公克) Fat (g)	醣類 (公克) CHO (g)
豆腐 Bean Curd Squares	3 塊 PC.	300	195	19.2	12.6	5.4
蝦仁 Shelled Shrimp		30	26.1	5.52	0.21	0.12
豌豆仁 Cooked Snow Peas		30	95.4	6.93	0.27	16.95
油 Cooking Oil	2 大匙 T.	30	270	—	30	—
糖 Sugar	½ 小匙 t.	2.5	10	—	—	2.5
太白粉 Cornstarch	½ 大匙 T.	7.5	25.3	0.1	0.02	6
合計 Total			622	31.75	43.1	31
一人份 Per Serving			104	5.3	7.2	5.2

材料：

豆腐‥‥‥‥3塊（300公克）
熟洋芋泥‥‥‥‥‥80公克
油‥‥‥‥‥‥1⅓大匙

① {
蝦仁（切丁）‥‥80公克
魠仔魚‥‥‥‥100公克
金菇（切小段）80公克
生香菇（切丁）‥‥‥‥
‥‥‥‥‥120公克
絞肉‥‥‥‥‥‥75公克
}

② {
高湯‥‥‥‥‥‥‥½杯
醬油、太白粉各1小匙
塩‥‥‥‥‥‥‥⅛小匙
}

③ {
蛋白‥‥1個（30公克）
塩‥‥‥‥‥‥‥¼小匙
胡椒粉‥‥‥‥‥⅛小匙
}

④ {
高湯‥‥‥‥‥‥‥1杯
太白粉‥‥‥‥‥2小匙
醬油‥‥‥‥‥‥1小匙
糖‥‥‥‥‥‥‥¼小匙
塩‥‥‥‥‥‥‥⅛小匙
}

❶鍋熱入油1大匙，炒香①料，再入②料略煮，盛起待冷
❷將豆腐壓碎入洋芋泥、上述❶料及③料一起拌勻後，放入已抹油（⅓大匙）的蒸碗中，以中火蒸20分鐘取出，倒扣於深盤中。
❸將④料燒開，淋於豆腐上即成。

INGREDIENTS:

3 (300g/10½ oz)		Bean Curd Squares
80 g (2⅘ oz)		Cooked Mashed Potatoes
1⅓ T.		Cooking Oil
①	80g (2⅘ oz)	Diced Shelled Shrimp
	100g (3½ oz)	Baby Fish
	80g (2⅘ oz)	Chopped Golden Mushrooms
	120g (4⅕ oz)	Diced Fresh Black Mushrooms
	75g (2⅗ oz)	Ground Pork
②	½ c.	Soup Stock
	1 t. each:	Soysauce, Cornstarch
	⅛ t.	Salt
③	1 (30g/1 oz)	Egg White
	¼ t.	Salt
	⅛ t.	Pepper
④	1 c.	Soup Stock
	2 t.	Cornstarch
	1 t.	Soysauce
	¼ t.	Sugar
	⅛ t.	Salt

❶ Heat wok, add 1 T. oil and stir-fry ① until fragrant. Add ② and simmer for a few minutes. Remove and allow to cool.
❷ Mash bean curd squares and mix with mashed potatoes. Stir in all ingredients from Step ❶, then blend in ③. Mix well. Grease medium-sized bowl with ⅓ T. oil and pour in mixed batter. Steam over medium heat for 20 minutes. When done, secure a deep platter face-down over top of bowl and turn over.
❸ Bring ④ to a boil, pour over bean curd mixture and serve.

項目 Item 材料 Material	份量・重量 （公克） Unit/Wt. (g)	熱 量 （卡） Energy (Cal.)	蛋白質 （公克） Prot. (g)	脂 肪 （公克） Fat (g)	醣 類 （公克） CHO (g)
豆腐 Bean Curd Squares	300	195	19.2	12.6	5.4
洋芋 Pre-Cooked Mashed Potato	80	60	1.84	0.08	13.52
蝦仁 Diced Shelled Shrimp	80	69.6	14.72	0.56	0.32
魠仔魚 Baby Fish	100	98	20	1.3.	0.1
金菇 Chopped Golden Mushroom	80	12.8	2.4	0.4	2.88
生香菇 Diced Fresh Black Mushroom	120	25.8	·2.6	0.34	11.8
絞肉 Ground Pork	75	411.8	9.23	41.1	—
油 Cooking Oil	1⅓大匙T. 20	180	—	20	—
蛋白 Egg White	1個PC. 30	14.4	3.03	0.03	0.24
太白粉 Cornstarch	2小匙t. 10	33.7	0.13	0.03	8
合 計 Total		1101	73.2	76.4	42.3
一人份 Per Serving		184	12.2	12.7	7.1

永結同心 Stir-Fried Beancurd Knots with Vegetables

6人份
serves 6

材料：

千張結(圖1)……160公克
熟紅蘿蔔片…… 100公克
熟草菇………… 100公克
乾髮菜(圖2) ……1大匙
(約1公克)
蔥末……………… 1大匙
水……………………… 2杯
蘇打粉……………¼小匙
油…………………… 1大匙
① 糖……………¾小匙
　 塩……………⅓小匙
　 胡椒粉………¼小匙
② 太白粉、水各½大匙

❶水2杯燒開入蘇打粉，再入千張結煮約3分鐘，撈起以冷水漂涼備用。

❷髮菜用清水浸泡10分鐘後，撈起備用。

❸鍋熱入油1大匙炒香蔥末，再下草菇、髮菜、紅蘿蔔片、千張結及①料，續煮2分鐘後淋下②料勾芡即成。

INGREDIENTS:

160g (5½ oz)	Bean Curd Knots (Illust. ①)
100g (3½ oz)	Cooked Sliced Carrots
100g (3½ oz)	Cooked Straw Mushrooms
1 T./1g	Dried Black Moss (Illust. ②)
1 T.	Minced Green Onion
2 c.	Water
¼ t.	Baking Soda
1 T.	Cooking Oil
① ¾ t.	Sugar
⅓ t.	Salt
¼ t.	Pepper
② ½ T. each:	Cornstarch, Water - mix

❶ Boil 2 c. water, add ¼ t. baking soda and cook bean curd knots for 3 minutes. Remove and rinse with cold water until cool. Set aside.

❷ Soak dried black moss in water for 10 minutes. Remove and drain.

❸ Heat wok, add 1 T. oil and stir-fry minced green onions until fragrant. Mix in straw mushrooms, pre-soaked sliced carrots, bean curd knots and ① (in that order). Cook for 2 minutes and add ② to thicken. Mix and serve.

項目 Item / 材料 Material	份量，重量 (公克) Unit/Wt. (g)	熱量 (卡) Energy (Cal.)	蛋白質 (公克) Prot. (g)	脂肪 (公克) Fat (g)	醣類 (公克) CHO (g)
千張結 Bean Curd Knots	160	745.6	82.72	40.16	17.92
胡蘿蔔 Cooked Sliced Carrots	100	37	1.0	0.4	8.0
草菇 Cooked Straw Mushrooms	100	28	3	0.3	3.2
糖 Sugar	¾ 小匙 t. 3.75	15	—	—	3.75
太白粉 Cornstarch	½ 大匙 T. 7.5	25.3	0.1	0.02	6
油 Cooking Oil	1 大匙 T. 15	135	—	15	—
合計 Total		986	86.8	55.9	38.9
一人份 Per Serving		164	14.5	9.3	6.5

材料：

白豆干(切絲)…… 120公克
香菇(泡軟切絲)……20公克
金菇………… 100公克
紫菜………… 4張
油………… 2大匙
麵糊：麵粉、水… 各2大匙
洋菇、青江菜… 各100公克
熟紅蘿蔔片、熟筍片………
…………各50公克

麻油…………… 1小匙
①{ 醬油露………… 1/2大匙
　 糖………… 1/2小匙
②{ 水………… 1杯
　 醬油露………… 1 1/2大匙
　 味精………… 1/4小匙
③{ 水………… 1大匙
　 太白粉………… 1小匙

❶鍋熱入油1大匙，將豆干絲、香菇絲、金菇入鍋拌炒，並以
　①料調味後，盛盤待涼，分成4份，分別以紫菜捲成筒狀
　(圖1)，以麵糊封口(圖2)。
❷鍋熱入油1大匙，將包好的紫菜捲入鍋略煎後，盛起切塊，
　餘油留鍋備用。
❸另鍋水燒開後，將洋菇、青江菜、紅蘿蔔片、筍片川燙撈
　出，用冷水漂涼，瀝乾水份備用。
❹留鍋之餘油燒熱，放入洋菇、青江菜、紅蘿蔔片、筍片略
　炒，隨入②料，燒煮至湯汁剩1/2杯時，將材料撈起置盤，
　再將切好的紫菜捲置材料上，洒上麻油，餘汁以③料勾芡
　，淋於紫菜捲上即成。

INGREDIENTS:

120g (4 oz)	Shredded Pressed Bean Curd
20g (2/3 oz)	Pre-Soaked and Shredded Dried Black Mushrooms
100g (3 1/2 oz)	Golden Mushrooms
4 sheets	Dried Pressed Seaweed (Nori)
2 T.	Cooking Oil

Flour Paste: 2 T. each: Flour, Water – mix

100g (3 1/2 oz)	Button Mushrooms
100g (3 1/2 oz)	Chinese Green Cabbage (Bok Choy)
50g (1 3/4 oz)	Cooked Sliced Carrots
50g (1 3/4 oz)	Cooked Sliced Bamboo Shoots
1 t.	Sesame Oil

① { 1/2 T. Soysauce
　 { 1/2 t. Sugar
② { 1 c. Water
　 { 1 1/2 T. Soysauce
③ { 1 T. Water } mix
　 { 1 t. Cornstarch }

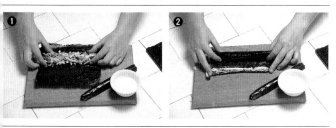

❶ Heat wok and add 1 T. oil. Stir-fry shredded pressed bean curd, black mushrooms and golden mushrooms. Mix and season with ①. Stir-fry, remove and allow to cool. Divide into 4 equal portions. Place a portion on each sheet of pressed seaweed and wrap into rolls (Illust. ①). Close openings with flour paste (Illust. ②).
❷ Re-heat wok and add 1 T. oil. Gently fry seaweed rolls, remove and cut into bite-size pieces. Retain oil in wok.
❸ Scald button mushrooms, cabbage, sliced carrots and bamboo shoots in boiling water. Remove and rinse until cool. Drain and set aside.
❹ Re-heat wok with retained oil. Stir-fry vegetables from Step ❸ and mix in ②. Simmer until sauce is reduced to 1/2 cup. Retain sauce in wok and place vegetables on serving plate. Arrange pre-cooked seaweed rolls on top of vegetables and sprinkle with 1 t. sesame oil. Re-heat retained sauce in wok and bring to a boil. Thicken with ③; pour sauce on rolls and serve.

項目 Item 材料 Material	份量，重量 (公克) Unit/Wt. (g)		熱量 (卡) Energy (Cal.)	蛋白質 (公克) Prot. (g)	脂肪 (公克) Fat (g)	醣類 (公克) CHO (g)
白豆腐干 Shredded Pressed Bean Curd	120		120	11.64	7.92	3.24
香菇 Mushrooms	20		25.8	2.6	0.34	11.8
金針菇 Golden Mushrooms	100		16	3	0.5	3.6
紫菜 Dried Pressed Seaweed	8		18.1	2.272	0.06	3.38
油 Cooking Oil	2 大匙 T.	30	270	—	30	—
洋菇 Button Mushrooms	100		16	3	0.5	3.6
青江菜 Chinese Green Cabbage	100		14	2	0.1	2.2
紅蘿蔔 Sliced Carrot	50		18.5	0.5	0.2	4
筍 Bamboo Shoots	50		43	4.55	0.6	7.55
麵粉 Flour	2 大匙 T.	30	101.85	3.09	0.41	21.9
麻油 Sesame Oil	1 小匙 t.	5	45	—	5	—
合計 Total			688	32.7	45.6	61.3
一人份 Per Serving			115	5.5	7.6	10.2

材料：

豆腐‥‥‥‥4塊（400公克）
乾香菇‥‥‥ 3朵（24公克）
青江菜‥‥‥‥‥ 250公克
炸油‥‥‥‥‥‥‥‥ 3杯

① { 水‥‥‥‥‥‥‥¼杯
　　醬油‥‥‥‥‥½大匙
　　糖‥‥‥‥‥‥1小匙

② { 醬油‥‥‥‥ 1½大匙
　　味精‥‥‥‥‥⅛小匙
③ 塩、味精‥‥各⅛小匙
④ { 水‥‥‥‥‥‥ 1大匙
　　太白粉‥‥‥‥1小匙

❶香菇泡軟去蒂入①料蒸10分鐘取出切成12片，餘汁加②料備用，豆腐每塊切成3長塊，炸油燒開，將豆腐炸成金黃色撈起，備用。

❷青江菜先川燙，鍋熱入油1大匙，入青江菜及③料炒，盛盤備用。

❸將豆腐、香菇相互排列在碗內（圖1）；入香菇餘汁，以大火蒸20分鐘後，再將蒸汁倒出備用，豆腐、香菇扣在大盤上（圖2），盤邊以青江菜圍邊。

❹蒸汁以④料勾茨淋於豆腐、香菇上即成。

INGREDIENTS:

4 (400g/14 oz)		Bean Curd Squares
3 (24g/1 oz)		Dried Black Mushrooms
250g (8¾ oz)		Chinese Green Cabbage (Bok Choy)
3 c.		Cooking Oil (for deep-frying)
①	¼ c.	Water
	½ T.	Soysauce
	1 t.	Sugar
②	1½ T.	Soysauce
③	⅛ t.	Salt
④	1 T.	Water } mix
	1 t.	Cornstarch

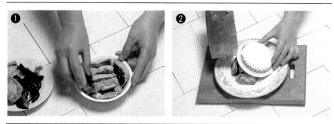

❶ Soak mushrooms until soft; rinse and trim off stems. In a small bowl, mix mushrooms with ① and steam for 10 minutes. Remove and slice into 1 pieces. Add ② to retained liquid and set aside. Slice each bean curd square vertically into 3 cm. lengths. Heat 3 c. oil and deep-fry bean curd pieces until golden brown. Remove and set aside.

❷ Parboil green cabbage in boiling water. Remove and drain. Heat wok, add 1 T. oil, and stir-fry green cabbage; season with ③, mix, remove and set aside.

❸ In a bowl, place sliced bean curd and mushroom side by side (Illust. ①). Pour in retained liquid from Step ❶, and steam over high heat for 20 minutes. Carefully pour out liquid from bowl and save for later use. Place serving plate face down on top of bowl, turn upside-down and remove bowl (Illust ②). Arrange pre-cooked green cabbage around rim.

❹ Re-heat retained liquid from Step ❸. Bring to a boil and thicken with ④. Sprinkle on bean curd and mushrooms.

項目 Item 材料 Material	份量，重量（公克）Unit/Wt. (g)		熱量（卡）Energy (Cal.)	蛋白質（公克）Prot. (g)	脂肪（公克）Fat (g)	醣類（公克）CHO (g)
豆腐 Bean Curd Squares	4 塊 PC.	400	260	25.6	16.8	7.2
青江菜 Chinese Green Cabbage		250	35	5	0.25	11
油 Cooking Oil	1 大匙 T.	15	135	—	15	—
糖 Sugar	1 小匙 t.	5	20	—	—	5
香菇 Dried Black Mushrooms		24	30.96	3.12	0.41	14.16
＊吸油 Cooking Oil Absorbed		65	585	—	65	—
合 計 Total			1066	33.7	97	102
一人份 Per Serving			178	5.6	16	17

韭菜豆腐 Bean Curd with Leeks

材料：
鷄丁（去皮）…… 120公克
韭菜（圖1）………100公克
豆腐………1塊（100公克）
蒜末… 1大匙（約10公克）
油……………… 1½大匙

① 高湯………………½杯
味噌（圖2）、番茄醬
醬油、麻油 各1大匙
糖…………… 1小匙

② 水…………… 1小匙
太白粉………½小匙

❶韭菜洗淨切2公分長段，豆腐切12小塊均備用。
❷鍋熱入油1大匙，將豆腐煎成兩面金黃色盛起。
❸鍋熱入油½大匙，依序炒鷄丁、蒜末再拌上①料後，
　下韭菜、豆腐最後入②料勾芡即成。

INGREDIENTS:

120g (4⅕ oz)	Diced Skinned Chicken
100g (3½ oz)	Leeks (Illust. ①)
1 (100g/3½ oz)	Bean Curd Square
1 T. (10g)	Minced Garlic
1½ T.	Cooking Oil

① ½ c. Soup Stock
1 T. each: Miso or Soy Bean Paste (Illust.②),
Ketchup, Soysauce, Sesame Oil
1 t. Sugar

② 1 t. Water
½ t. Cornstarch } mix

❶ Wash leeks and cut into 2 cm.-length segments. Cut bean curd into 12 small pieces. Set aside.
❷ Heat wok and add 1 T. oil. Gently fry bean curd pieces until both sides are golden brown. Remove.
❸ Re-heat wok and add ½ T. oil. Stir-fry diced chicken, then add minced garlic, followed by ①. Mix thoroughly and stir in leeks, then add bean curd to mixture. Thicken sauce with ②, remove and serve.

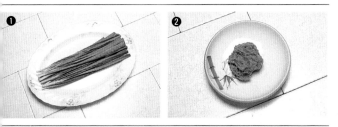

材料 Material	項目 Item 份量・重量 （公克） Unit/Wt. (g)	熱 量 （卡） Energy (Cal.)	蛋白質 （公克） Prot. (g)	脂 肪 （公克） Fat (g)	醣 類 （公克） CHO (g)
韭菜 Leek	100	17	2.2	0.4	2.2
豆腐 Bean Curd Square	100	65	6.4	4.2	1.8
鷄丁 Diced Chicken	120	204	37.8	3.6	—
油 Cooking Oil	1½ 大匙 T. 37.5	337.5	—	37.5	—
番茄醬 Ketchup	15	13.95	0.24	0.05	3.53
糖 Sugar	5	20	—	—	5
味噌 Miso or Soy Bean Paste	15	20.7	1.88	0.96	3.69
麻油 Sesame Oil	1 大匙 T. 15	135	—	15	—
合 計 Total		813	48.5	61.7	16.22
一人份 Per Serving		136	8.1	10.3	2.7

材料：

壽司豆腐皮6個（110公克）
干瓢………1捲（5公克）

① { 生香菇絲… 120公克
紅蘿蔔絲… 100公克
筍絲………100公克
肉絲………100公克
海帶絲………30公克 }

② { 高湯…………1
醬油………½大
酒…………1小
糖…………½小 }

③ { 高湯…………2
醬油………½大
糖、酒……各1小
塩…………¼小 }

❶將豆腐皮及干瓢入開水煮2分鐘使之軟化。
❷①料加②料煮軟，汁縮乾後分爲六等份備用，豆腐
切去三個邊，攤開，將1份餡（圖1）放入捲成筒狀，
干瓢綁牢兩端（圖2）。
❸③料燒開將豆腐皮捲放入煮約10分鐘，使入味，盛
，食時由每捲中間切成2份排盤。

INGREDIENTS:

6 pcs. (110g/3¾ oz)　Fried Bean Curd Skin
1 roll (5 g)　　　　　Dried Gourd Strip

① { 120g (4⅕ oz)　Shredded Fresh Black Mushroom
100g (3½ oz)　Shredded Carrots
100g (3½ oz)　Shredded Bamboo Shoots
100g (3½ oz)　Shredded Pork
30g (1 oz)　　Pre-Soaked Shredded Kelp
　　　　　　　　(Seaweed) }

② { 1 c.　　Soup Stock
½ T.　　Soysauce
1 t.　　Cooking Wine
½ t.　　Sugar }

③ { 2 c.　　Soup Stock
½ T.　　Soysauce
1 t. each:　Sugar, Cooking Wine
¼ t.　　Salt }

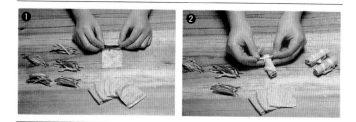

❶ Cook bean curd skin and gourd strip in boiling
water until soft (about 20 minutes).
❷ To make filling, bring ② to a boil, add all in
gredients in ① and cook until soft (there should
be no liquid left). Divide into 6 portions and se
aside. Cut off 3 sides of each bean curd skin
and spread out. Place a portion of filling onto
each bean curd skin and roll into cylinders (Illust
①). Secure both ends by tying with gourd strip
(Illust. ②).
❸ Bring ③ to a boil, add rolls and cook until flavor
absorbed (about 10 minutes). Remove, cut into
halves and serve.

材料 Material	項目 Item 份量・重量 （公克） Unit/Wt. (g)	熱 量 （卡） Energy (Cal.)	蛋白質 （公克） Prot. (g)	脂 肪 （公克） Fat (g)	糖 類 （公克） CHO (g)
海帶絲 Pre-Soaked Shredded Kelp	30	6.9	0.3	0.06	1.59
筍絲 Shredded Bamboo Shoot	100	19	2.6	0.5	2.4
紅蘿蔔 Shredded Carrot	100	37	1.0	0.4	8.0
肉 Shredded Pork	100	347	14.6	31.6	—
生香菇 Shredded Fresh Black Mushrooms	120	25.8	2.6	0.34	11.8
豆腐包 Bean Curd Skin	110	512.6	56.8	27.6	12.3
糖 Sugar	1½ 小匙 t. 7.5	67.5	—	7.5	—
合 計 Total		978	78	61	43.1
一人份 Per Serving		163	13	10.1	7.2

海帶芽蒸豆腐　Steamed Eggs with Kelp

材料：

蛋…………4個(250公克)
海帶芽(圖1)…… 10公克
油………少許(約½小匙)

① { 高湯………… 1¾杯
醬油、酒… 各1小匙
醋、塩、糖…各½小匙 }

② { 高湯…………¾杯
醬油………… 1大匙
糖、酒、醋各½小匙 }

❶海帶芽川燙，撈起切4～5公分長段。
❷分別將①、②料煮沸盛起放涼備用。
❸蛋4個打勻，拌入①料，並以濾網濾過，即為蛋汁。
❹方形便當盒內抹油，將蛋汁倒入便當盒裡，並拌入切好的海帶芽(圖2)，入蒸籠先以大火蒸2～3分鐘後改小火 再蒸10分鐘。
❺吃時倒扣盤上淋上②料調味即成。
■此道菜可冷食亦可熱食。

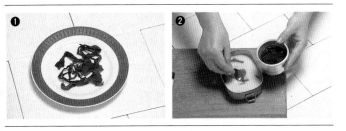

INGREDIENTS:

4 (250g/8⅙ oz)		Eggs
10g		Kelp (Seaweed) (Illust. ①)
½ t.		Cooking Oil
①	1¾ c.	Soup Stock
	1 t. each:	Soysauce, Cooking Wine
	½ t. each:	Sugar, Vinegar, Salt
②	¾ c.	Soup Stock
	1 T.	Soysauce
	½ t. each:	Sugar, Cooking Wine, Vinegar

❶ Scald kelp in boiling water; remove and cut into 4-5 cm. lengths.
❷ Separately bring ① and ② to boiling. Keep in separate bowls and allow to cool.
❸ Beat 4 eggs until smooth; blend in pre-boiled ①, and pass mixture through a strainer.
❹ Lightly grease a loaf pan with ½ t. oil. Pour in egg mixture and stir in kelp (Illust. ②). Steam over high heat for 2-3 minutes. Lower heat, and continue to steam for an additional 10 minutes.
❺ To serve, release on to platter, slice and sprinkle with pre-boiled seasoning ②.
■ May be served hot or cold.

材料 Material	份量，重量 Unit/Wt. (g)	熱量 Energy (Cal.)	蛋白質 Prot. (g)	脂肪 Fat (g)	糖類 CHO (g)
蛋 Egg	4 個 PC. 250	432.5	31.25	32	2.
海帶芽 Kelp	10	2.3	0.1	0.02	0.53
油 Cooking Oil	½ 小匙 t. 2.5	22.5	—	2.5	—
糖 Sugar	1 小匙 t. 5	20	—	5	—
合 計 Total		477	32.4	39.5	2.53
一人份 Per Serving		80	5.4	6.6	0.4

扒素三白 Bean Curd With Mushrooms and Asparagus

材料：

未炸豆包(圖1)‥‥‥‥3片
（約120公克）

綠蘆筍‥‥‥‥‥‥‥90公克
鮑魚菇(圖2)‥‥‥‥120公克
葱段‥‥‥‥‥‥‥‥1枝
油‥‥‥‥‥‥‥‥1⅓大匙

① { 水‥‥‥‥‥‥ 1½杯
　　酒‥‥‥‥‥‥ ½大匙

② { 塩‥‥‥‥‥‥ ½小匙
　　味精‥‥‥‥‥ ¼小匙

③ { 水‥‥‥‥‥‥ 1½大匙
　　太白粉‥‥‥‥ 1大匙

❶未炸豆包切3×4公分片狀，鮑魚菇切斜片，蘆筍切斜段川燙漂涼，備用。

❷鍋熱入油1大匙爆香葱段隨入①料煮開，再放入鮑魚菇煮1分鐘後，入②料及豆包同煮至開，拿掉葱段並放入蘆筍，以③料勾成薄稠狀，起鍋前淋上熟油⅓大匙即成。

INGREDIENTS:

3 pcs. (120g/4 oz)	Layered Bean Curd Skin (Illust. ①)
90g (3 oz)	Green Asparagus
120g (4⅙ oz)	Abalone Mushrooms (Illust. ②)
1 stalk	Green Onion (cut into segments)
1 ⅓ T.	Cooking Oil

① { 1½ c.　　　Water
　 ½ T.　　　Cooking Wine

② { ½ t.　　　Salt

③ { 1½ T.　　Water　　} mix
　 1 T.　　　Cornstarch

❶ Cut layered bean curd into 3×4cm. slices. Holding knife at an angle, slice mushrooms and cut asparagus into segments. Scald all 3 ingredients in boiling water. Remove and allow to cool.

❷ Heat wok; add 1 T. oil; and stir-fry green onion segments until fragrant. Stir in ① and bring to a boil. Add sliced mushrooms and cook for 1 minute. Mix in bean curd slices with ② and return to boiling. Remove and discard green onion segments. Add asparagus, stir, and mix in ③. When thickened, drizzle with ⅓ T. hot oil and serve.

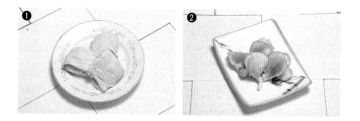

材料 Material	項目 Item 份量，重量 (公克) Unit/Wt.(g)	熱 量 (卡) Energy (Cal.)	蛋白質 (公克) Prot.(g)	脂 肪 (公克) Fat(g)	醣 類 (公克) CHO(g)
豆包 Layered Bean Curd Skin	120	552	62.04	30.12	13.44
綠蘆筍 Green Asparagus	90	50.4	3.6	—	9
鮑魚菇 Abalone Mushrooms	120	33.6	3.6	0.36	3.84
油 Cooking Oil	1⅓ 大匙 T. 20	180	0	20	0
太白粉 Cornstarch	1 大匙 T. 15	50.55	0.19	0.04	12
合 計 Total		866.6	69.4	50.5	38.3
一人份 Per Serving		144	11.5	8.4	6.4

材料：

豆腐⋯⋯⋯3塊（300公克）
洋葱丁⋯⋯⋯⋯150公克
絞肉⋯⋯⋯⋯⋯100公克
熟紅蘿蔔絲⋯⋯⋯60公克
青椒絲⋯⋯⋯⋯20公克
麵粉⋯⋯⋯⋯⋯3大匙
油⋯⋯⋯⋯⋯⋯2大匙

① ┤ 塩⋯⋯⋯⋯⋯¾小匙
胡椒粉⋯⋯⋯¼小匙
蛋⋯⋯1個（50公克）

② ┤ 高湯⋯⋯⋯⋯⅔杯
番茄醬⋯⋯⋯4大匙
黑醋⋯⋯⋯1½小匙
糖⋯⋯⋯⋯⅔小匙

❶鍋熱入油½大匙，炒香洋葱丁，盛盤待冷。
❷豆腐用紗布吸乾水份（圖1）入大碗中攪碎，再入絞肉、洋葱丁及①料拌勻，分成六份，一一做成圓球狀（圖2），外沾少許麵粉，即爲漢堡豆腐。
❸鍋熱入油1½大匙，將漢堡豆腐放入，一一壓成約1公分厚的圓餅狀，煎至兩面金黃，再入②料、青椒絲及紅蘿蔔絲，煮至湯汁變成濃稠狀，即可起鍋排盤。

INGREDIENTS:

3 (300g/10½ oz)	Bean Curd Squares
150g (5¼ oz)	Chopped Onions
100g (3½ oz)	Ground Pork
60g (2 oz)	Shredded Cooked Carrots
20g (¾ oz)	Shredded Green Bell Pepper
3 T.	Flour
2 T.	Cooking Oil

① ┤ ¾ t. — Salt
¼ t. — Pepper
1 (50g) — Egg

② ┤ ⅔ c. — Soup Stock
4 T. — Ketchup
1½ t. — Dark Vinegar
⅔ t. — Sugar

❶ Heat wok, add ½ T. oil, and stir-fry chopped onions until fragrant. Remove and let cool.

❷ Pat bean curd squares dry with paper towel or gauze (Illust. ①). Place in a bowl and mash. Stir in ground pork, pre-cooked onions and ①. Mix well and divide into 6 portions. Roll into 6 balls (Illust. ②) and dredge each ball with flour.

❸ Heat wok or frying pan and add 1½ T. oil. Add bean curd patties and using spatula, flatten until 1 cm. thick. Fry both sides until golden brown. Then add ②, followed by shredded green pepper and carrots. Simmer until sauce is thickened.

❶

❷

項目 Item 材料 Material	份量，重量（公克）Unit/Wt. (g)	熱量（卡）Energy (Cal.)	蛋白質（公克）Prot. (g)	脂肪（公克）Fat (g)	醣類（公克）CHO (g)
豆腐 Bean Curd Squares	3 塊 PC. 300	195	19.2	12.6	5.4
洋葱 Chopped Onion	150	37.5	1.35	0.6	7.5
絞肉 Ground Pork	100	549	12.3	54.8	—
青椒 Shredded Green Bell Pepper	20	32	0.2	0.04	0.66
胡蘿蔔 Shredded Cooked Carrot	60	22.2	0.6	0.24	4.8
蛋 Egg	1 個 PC. 50	86.5	6.25	6.4	0.4
糖 Sugar	⅔ 小匙 t. 3.3	13.2	—	—	3.3
番茄醬 Ketchup	4 大匙 T. 60	55.8	0.96	0.18	14.1
油 Cooking Oil	2 大匙 T. 30	270	0	30	0
麵粉 Flour	3 大匙 T. 45	152.8	4.64	0.6	32.9
合 計 Total		1414	45.5	105.5	69.1
一人份 Per Serving		236	7.6	17.6	11.5

同心豆包捲 Vegetarian Rolls

材料：
未炸豆包(圖1)…420公克
菠菜……………60公克
紅蘿蔔…半條(300公克)
麵｜水………3大匙
糊｜麵粉……2大匙
油……………2大匙

① 高湯…………… 1杯
｜酒、醬油…… 2大匙
糖…………… 1小匙
塩…………… ¼小匙

② 開水、醬油 各1大匙
蒜末………… 1小匙
麻油………… ½小匙
塩、糖…… 各¼小匙

❶ 紅蘿蔔去皮，直切成兩半，入①料煮熟後連湯浸泡約20分鐘，取出切長條(約0.5×8公分)，菠菜洗淨川燙，撈起漂涼，瀝乾水份後，切8公分長段，分成6份備用。

❷ 豆包用手輕輕撕開，將菠菜舖上約5公分寬大小，中心再放上1條紅蘿蔔捲成圓筒狀，封口以麵糊粘住(圖2)，如此將所有材料做成6捲。

❸ 鍋熱入油2大匙，將豆包捲入鍋以中火煎至外皮呈金黃色盛起，切斜段排盤，食時沾調勻的②料即成。

INGREDIENTS:

420g (14¾ oz)	Layered Bean Curd Skin (Illust. ①)
60g (2 oz)	Spinach
½ (300g/10½ oz)	Carrot
Flour Paste: { 3 T. Water / 2 T. Flour } mix	
2 T.	Cooking Oil

①
1 c.	Soup Stock
2 T. each:	Cooking Wine, Soysauce
1 t.	Sugar
¼ t.	Salt

②
1 T. each:	Water, Soysauce
1 t.	Minced Garlic
½ t.	Sesame Oil
¼ t. each:	Salt, Sugar

❶ Pare half a carrot and split vertically into 2. Boil in ① until cooked, turn off heat and allow to soak for 20 minutes. Remove and cut into 0.5×8 cm. lengths. Wash spinach and scald in boiling water. Remove and let cool by rinsing in cold water. Drain and cut into 8-cm. lengths Divide into 6 portions.

❷ Gently spread out layered bean curd skins. Lay 1 portion spinach (width of spinach should be about 5 cm.), then place 1 carrot segment in center. Roll and close ends with flour paste (Illust. ②). Make 6 rolls.

❸ Heat wok and add 2 T. oil. Gently fry bean curd rolls over medium heat until skin appears golden brown. Remove and cut into bite-size pieces at an angle. Arrange on platter and serve with seasoning sauce ② (separately in a small dish).

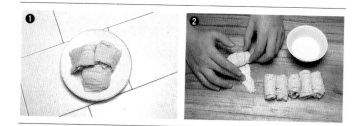

項目 Item 材料 Material	份量，重量 (公克) Unit/Wt. (g)	熱量 (卡) Energy (Cal.)	蛋白質 (公克) Prot. (g)	脂肪 (公克) Fat (g)	醣類 (公克) CHO (g)
豆包(未炸) Layered Bean Curd Skin	420	730	70	50	—
菠菜 Spinach	600	96	13.8	1.2	14.4
紅蘿蔔 Carrot	300	111	3	1.2	24
糖 Sugar	1¼ 小匙 t. 6.25	25	—	—	6.25
麻油 Sesame Oil	½ 小匙 t. 2.5	22.5	—	2.5	—
油 Cooking Oil	2 大匙 T. 30	270	—	30	—
麵粉 Flour	2 大匙 T. 30	102	2.1	0.4	22
合計 Total		1356	88.9	85.3	66.7
一人份 Per Serving		226	14.8	14.2	11.1

蔬菜豆腐煎餅 Bean Curd and Vegetable Pancake

材料：

豆腐·········4塊（400公克）
蛋··········2個（100公克）
熟胡蘿蔔丁········60公克
熟青豆仁·········30公克
香菇··········20公克
油············ 2大匙

① 醬油·········· 1大匙
糖············ 1小匙

② 太白粉········ 1大匙
糖············ 2小匙
酒············ 1小匙
塩···········³⁄₄小匙

❶將香菇泡軟去蒂切丁，留汁½杯備用，蛋打散備用。
❷將熟胡蘿蔔丁、香菇丁、香菇汁及①料煮至湯汁收乾，盛盤待冷。
❸豆腐以乾布擠乾水份，置大碗中壓碎，入蛋液、上述❷料、熟青豆仁及調味料②拌勻。
❹鍋熱入油2大匙，將蔬菜、豆腐倒入煎至兩面金黃，起鍋切塊排盤。

INGREDIENTS:

4 (400g/14 oz)		Bean Curd Squares
2 (100g/3½ oz)		Eggs
60g (2 oz)		Cooked Diced Carrots
30g (1 oz)		Cooked Green Peas
20g (²⁄₃ oz)		Dried Black Mushrooms
2 T.		Cooking Oil
①	1 T.	Soysauce
	1 t.	Sugar
②	1 T.	Cornstarch
	2 t.	Sugar
	1 t.	Cooking Wine
	¾ t.	Salt

❶ Rinse black mushrooms and soak until soft. Remove stems and dice. Retain ½ c. liquid from soaking. Beat 2 eggs and set aside.

❷ In a saucepan, heat ½ c. liquid retained from soaking mushrooms; add diced carrots, mushrooms and ①; and simmer until no liquid remains. Place on platter and allow to cool.

❸ Dry bean curd squares by squeezing gently with cheesecloth or paper towel, then place in a large bowl and mash thoroughly. Stir in eggs, ②, and pre-cooked green peas, followed by pre-cooked diced carrots and mushrooms from Step ❷. Mix well.

❹ Heat wok or skillets; add 2 T. oil; and pour in batter from Step ❸. Gently fry both sides over low heat until golden brown. Slice and serve.

項目 Item 材料 Material	份量·重量 (公克) Unit/Wt. (g)		熱量 (卡) Energy (Cal.)	蛋白質 (公克) Prot. (g)	脂肪 (公克) Fat (g)	醣類 (公克) CHO (g)
豆腐 Bean Curd	4 塊 PC.	400	260	25.6	16.8	7.2
蛋 Egg	2 個 PC.	100	173	12.5	12.8	0.8
青豆仁 Cooked Green Beans		30	95.4	6.93	0.27	10.95
紅蘿蔔 Cooked Carrots		60	22.2	0.6	0.24	4.8
香菇 Black Mushrooms		20	25.8	2.6	0.34	11.8
糖 Sugar	1 大匙 T.	15	60	—	—	15
太白粉 Cornstarch	1 大匙 T.	15	50.55	0.19	0.04	12
油 Cooking Oil	2 大匙 T.	30	270	0	30	0
合計 Total			957	48.4	60.5	68.6
一人份 Per Serving			160	8.1	10.1	11.4

材料：

青江菜⋯⋯⋯⋯⋯ 150公克
蘆筍(罐頭)⋯⋯⋯ 150公克
小紅番茄⋯⋯(3個)120公克
草菇⋯⋯⋯⋯⋯ 150公克
油⋯⋯⋯⋯⋯⋯ 1大匙
① { 塩⋯⋯⋯⋯⋯ ¼小匙
   { 味精⋯⋯⋯⋯ ⅛小匙

② { 高湯⋯⋯⋯⋯ ½
   { 醬油露⋯⋯ 2小
③ 太白粉、水各1½小
④ { 高湯⋯⋯⋯⋯ ½
   { 塩⋯⋯⋯⋯ ½小
   { 味精、酒、麻油⋯
   { ⋯⋯⋯各⅛小
⑤ 太白粉、水各1½小

❶青江菜洗淨對切，川燙，撈出漂冷水，瀝乾備用。
❷鍋熱入油1大匙，入青江菜及①料，炒至熟，即可取
　排盤。
❸水2杯燒開，入蘆筍及番茄川燙1～2分鐘，撈出，將
　筍排盤，番茄先去皮，再對切排盤。
❹草菇川燙，撈出備用，②料煮開後入已川燙之草菇
　1分鐘，再用③料勾芡排盤中央。
❺④料煮沸，以⑤料勾芡，淋在蔬菜上即成。

INGREDIENTS:

150g (5¼ oz)	Chinese Green Cabbage (Bok Choy)
150g (5¼ oz)	Asparagus
3 (120g/4⅛)	Small Ripe Tomatoes
150g (5¼ oz)	Straw Mushrooms
1 T.	Cooking Oil
① ¼ t.	Salt
② { ½ c.	Soup Stock
{ 2 t.	Soysauce
③ 1½ t. each:	Water, Cornstarch - mix
④ { ½ c.	Soup Stock
{ ½ t.	Salt
{ ⅛ t. each:	Cooking Wine, Sesame Oil
⑤ 1½ t. each:	Water, Cornstarch - mix

❶ Wash green cabbage, halve each stalk and scald in boiling water. Remove and rinse in cold water; drain and set aside.
❷ Heat wok, add 1 T. oil and stir-fry green cabbage. Season with ① and stir until cooked. Remove and arrange on platter.
❸ Snap off tips of asparagus. Cook asparagus and tomatoes in boiling water 1-2 minutes. Remove arrange asparagus on platter; Peel tomatoes, cut into halves; and arrange on platter.
❹ Scald straw mushrooms in boiling water, remove and set aside. Bring ② to a boil; stir in pre-scalded straw mushrooms and cook for 1 minute. Pour in ③ to thicken. Remove and place in center of platter.
❺ Bring ④ to a boil and thicken with ⑤. Sprinkle over vegetables on platter and serve.

項目 Item 材料 Material	份量，重量 Unit/Wt. (公克)(g)	熱 量 Energy (卡)(Cal.)	蛋白質 Prot. (公克)(g)	脂 肪 Fat (公克)(g)	醣 類 CHO (公克)(g)
青江菜 Chinese Green Cabbage	150	21	3	0.15	3.3
蘆筍 Asparagus	150	84	6	—	15
番茄 Small Ripe Tomatoes	120	21.6	0.84	0.36	4.2
草菇 Straw Mushrooms	150	12	4.5	0.45	4.8
油 Cooking Oil	1 大匙 T. 15	135	0	15	0
麻油 Sesame Oil	⅛ 小匙 t. 0.625	5.625	0	0.625	0
太白粉 Cornstarch	1 大匙 T. 15	50.5	0.18	0.03	12
合 計 Total		330	14.5	16.6	39.3
一人份 Per Serving		55	2.4	2.8	6.6

酸梅高麗菜捲　Cabbage Rolls With Sour Plums

6人份
serves 6

材料：

高麗菜	200公克
醃泡酸梅	4顆
塩	⅛小匙

① ｛ 醬油、碎柴魚片、酒… 各1大匙
　　 醃梅汁 … ½小匙
　　 糖 … ¼小匙

❶高麗菜整棵用水煮至葉軟（約3分鐘）（圖1），撈起剝6片
　高麗菜葉（200公克）趁熱撒上塩，去中間硬梗（圖2）。

❷酸梅去籽，剁碎，入①料用慢火煮至汁收乾即可放入
　盤中，分為6等份備用。

❸高麗菜葉攤開，捲入梅肉餡1份，捲成圓柱狀，然後切
　成2公分長段排盤即可。

INGREDIENTS:

200g (7 oz)	Cabbage
4	Preserved Sour Plums
⅛ t.	Salt

① ｛ 1 T. each: Soysauce, Shredded Stock Fish, Cooking Wine
　　 ½ t. Liquid from Preserved Sour Plums
　　 ¼ t. Sugar

❶ Boil cabbage until leaves are softened (about 3 minutes) (Illust. ①). Remove and drain. Tear off 6 leaves (net weight app. 200g/7 oz). While hot, sprinkle with ⅛ t. salt. Trim off hard stems. (Illust. ②).

❷ Pit plums and mince pulp; simmer in saucepan with ① over low heat until almost dry. Remove and divide into 6 portions.

❸ Spread out cabbage leaves. Place a portion of minced plum on each sheet and wrap into rolls. Slice into 2-cm. pieces. Arrange on a platter and serve.

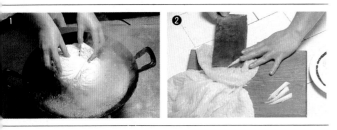

材料 Material	項目 Item 份量，重量（公克）Unit/Wt. (g)	熱 量（卡）Energy (Cal.)	蛋白質（公克）Prot. (g)	脂 肪（公克）Fat (g)	醣 類（公克）CHO (g)
高麗菜 Cabbage	200	34	3.8	0.2	6.2
油 Cooking Oil	1 大匙 T. 15	15	0	1	0
糖 Sugar	¼ 小匙 t. 1.25	5	—	—	1.25
合 計 Total		54	3.8	1.2	7.5
一人份 Per Serving		9	0.6	0.2	1.2

材料：

蓮藕	·············	100公克
葱	·············	100公克
胡蘿蔔	·············	100公克
油	·············	½大匙
①	蛋 ·············	3個(150公克)
	冷水 ·············	1¼杯
	麵粉 ·············	1杯
	塩 ·············	½小匙

❶ 蓮藕去皮，切0.5公分厚之薄片，川燙，撈起備用。切3公分長段，並縱切成粗絲。胡蘿蔔亦切3公分長粗絲。

❷ 將①料調勻即為麵糊。

❸ 平底鍋燒熱，油½大匙抹勻鍋面，並由外向內依序鋪上蓮藕片、胡蘿蔔絲及葱絲後(圖1)，淋上麵糊(圖2)，以小火慢煎成兩面金黃色的薄餅，盛起切塊即成

INGREDIENTS:

100g (3½ oz)	Lotus Roots
100g (3½ oz)	Green Onions
100g (3½ oz)	Carrots
½ T.	Cooking Oil
① 3 (150g/5¼ oz)	Eggs
1¼ c.	Water
1 c.	Flour
½ t.	Salt

❶ Rinse and pare lotus roots; cut into 0.5-cm. slice and scald in boiling water, remove and set aside. Cut green onions into 3-cm. lengths and shred vertically. Coarsely slice carrots into 3-cm. length and shred.

❷ To make batter, mix all ingredients in ①.

❸ Heat skillet and grease evenly with ½ T. oil. Place sliced lotus roots one by one in a large circle close to rim of skillet, then add shredded carrots in another circle closer to the center. Finally, place shredded green onions in the space left in the center (Illust. ①). Pour in pre-mixed batter (Illust. ②) and fry slowly over low heat until a thin pancake is formed. Fry both sides until golden brown. Remove, cut into 6 slices and serve.

材料 Material	項目 Item	份量，重量（公克）Unit/Wt.(g)	熱 量（卡）Energy (Cal.)	蛋白質（公克）Prot.(g)	脂 肪（公克）Fat (g)	醣 類（公克）CHO (g)
蓮藕 Louts Root		100	52	1.7	0.1	12
胡蘿蔔 Carrot		100	37	1.0	0.4	8.0
麵粉 Flour	1 杯 C. 150		507	16.7	1.8	108.6
蛋 Egg	3 個 PC. 150		259.5	18.75	19.2	1.2
油 Cooking Oil	½ 大匙 T. 7.5		67.5	0	7.5	0
葱 Green Onion		100	27	1.8	0.3	5.6
合 計 Total			950	40	29.3	135.4
一人份 Per Serving			158	6.7	4.9	22.6

蒜香白菜 · Tossed Nappa Cabbage

材料：

大白菜	250公克
蘋果（去皮）	200公克
木耳	30公克
蒜頭	15公克
塩	½小匙
① 醋	3大匙
糖	1大匙
塩	½小匙

❶大白菜切絲以½小匙塩揉過，出水後瀝乾備用。
❷木耳川燙切細絲。
❸蒜頭和蘋果均去皮磨碎放入①料中，拌入大白菜及木耳使其入味，食用時略擠水份，即可排盤。

INGREDIENTS:

250g (8⅘ oz)	Nappa Cabbage
200g (7 oz)	Pared Apples
30g (1 oz)	Dried Fungus (Black Wood Ear)
15g (½ oz)	Garlic Cloves
½ t.	Salt
① 3 T.	Vinegar
1 T.	Sugar
½ t.	Salt

❶ Cut cabbage into shreds and mix well with ½ t. salt. When water starts to seep through, squeeze and drain. Set aside.
❷ Scald wood ear in boiling water; remove hard stems and shred into thin strips.
❸ Grate garlic and apples and blend with ①. Mix in shredded cabbage and wood ear and allow to soak until flavor absorbed. Prior to serving, gently squeeze out excess liquid and toss on platter.

項目 Item 材料 Material	份量，重量 （公克） Unit/Wt. (g)	熱量 （卡） Energy (Cal.)	蛋白質 （公克） Prot. (g)	脂肪 （公克） Fat (g)	醣類 （公克） CHO (g)
白菜 Nappa Cabbage	250	35	3.25	0.5	6.25
木耳 Black Wood Ear	30	33.9	3.03	0.36	19.22
蘋果 Pared Apple	1個 PC. 200	78	0.6	0.6	19.6
糖 Sugar	1大匙 T. 15	60	—	—	1.5
合 計 Total		206.9	6.9	1.5	59.9
一人份 Per Serving		34	1.1	0.2	10

材料：

鮑魚菇……6朵（350公克）
青花菜1顆（淨重300公克）
葱……………………… 1支
薑……………………… 2片
油………………… 2½ 大匙

① ｛ 水…………………… ¼杯
　　 塩………………… ¼小匙
　　 味精……………… ⅛小匙

② ｛ 水………………… 1½杯
　　 醬油露……… 1大匙
　　 糖…………… 1小匙
　　 塩………… ½小匙
　　 味精…… ¼小匙

③ ｛ 水………… 1大匙
　　 太白粉…… 1小匙

❶鮑魚菇洗淨，去蒂每朵斜切成2片，青花菜切成小朵，水燒開將鮑魚菇及青花菜川燙，撈起漂涼瀝乾，葱切3公分長段備用。

❷鍋熱入油1大匙，將青花菜及①料入鍋拌炒後盛起排盤，再入1大匙油爆香葱薑，續入②料及鮑魚菇煮至湯汁剩½杯時，將葱薑撈起入青花菜略煮，再以③料勾成薄稠狀，起鍋前淋上½大匙熟油即可排盤。

INGREDIENTS:

6 (350g/12⅓ oz)		Abalone Mushrooms
1 (300g/10½ oz)		Broccoli
1 stalk		Green Onion
2 slices		Ginger
2½ T.		Cooking Oil
①	¼ c.	Water
	¼ t.	Salt
②	1½ c.	Water
	1 T.	Soysauce
	1 t.	Sugar
	½ t.	Salt
③	1 T.	Water } mix
	1 t.	Cornstarch }

❶ Wash mushrooms, remove stems and cut into halves at a slant. Wash broccoli and cut into bite-size pieces. Scald mushrooms and broccoli in boiling water, remove, rinse under running water until cooled and drain. Cut green onion into 3-cm. lengths and set aside.

❷ Heat wok; add 1 T. oil; and stir-fry broccoli with ①. Remove and set aside. Re-heat wok; add 1 T. oil and stir-fry green onion segments with ginger slices until fragrant. Stir in ②; add mushrooms; and allow to simmer until liquid is reduced to approximately ½ cup. Remove and discard green onion and ginger. Add broccoli and continue to stir. Thicken with mixture ③. Drizzle with ½ T. hot oil (heated separately) and serve on platter.

項目 Item 材料 Material	份量・重量 (公克) Unit/Wt. (g)	熱 量 (卡) Energy (Cal.)	蛋白質 (公克) Prot. (g)	脂 肪 (公克) Fat (g)	醣 類 (公克) CHO (g)
鮑魚菇 Abalone Mushrooms	350	98	10.5	1.05	11.2
青花菜 Broccoli	300	60	6.0	0.3	10.8
油 Cooking Oil	2½ 大匙 T. 37.5	337.5	0	37.5	0
糖 Sugar	1 小匙 t. 5	20	—	—	5
太白粉 Cornstarch	1 小匙 t. 5	16.85	0.06	0.01	4
合 計 Total		528	16.6	38.8	31
一人份 Per Serving		88	2.8	6.5	5.2

材料：
馬鈴薯························· 300公克
菠菜·························· 200公克
蛋 ·························50公克
① ⎰ 沙拉醬·······················½大匙
　⎱ 塩、胡椒粉、糖········各⅛小匙

❶菠菜川燙至熟即撈起漂冷水瀝乾水份，切成末。
❷馬鈴薯去皮切丁和蛋整個入鍋煮熟撈起，蛋去殼，蛋
　白切丁(圖1)，蛋黃壓碎(圖2)。
❸將菠菜末、馬鈴薯丁、蛋白丁和①料拌勻，最後撒上
　蛋黃末即成。

INGREDIENTS:

300g (10½ oz) Potatoes
200g (7 oz) Spinach
1 (50g/1¾ oz) Egg
① ⎰ ½ T. Mayonaise
　⎱ ⅛ t. each: Salt, Pepper, Sugar

❶ Wash spinach and boil until cooked; remove
and rinse with cold water; drain, squeeze out
excess water; and mince.
❷ Pare potatoes and dice. Place in water with 1
egg and boil until potatoes are well done and
egg is hard-boiled. Remove and drain. Peel egg;
dice egg-white (Illust. ①) and mash yolk (Illust. ②).
❸ Mix minced spinach, diced potatoes and egg-
white with ① and place on platter. Sprinkle
mashed egg-yolk and serve.

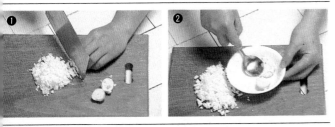

材料 Material	份量・重量 (公克) Unit/Wt. (g)	熱　量 (卡) Energy (Cal.)	蛋白質 (公克) Prot. (g)	脂　肪 (公克) Fat (g)	醣　類 (公克) CHO (g)
馬鈴薯 Potato	300	225	6.9	0.3	50.7
菠菜 Spinach	200	3.2	4.6	0.4	4.8
蛋 Egg	1 個 PC. 50	86.5	6.25	6.4	0.4
沙拉醬 Mayonaise	½ 大匙 T. 7.5	43.4	0.28	4.75	0.01
合　計 Total		386.9	18.0	11.9	55.9
一人份 Per Serving		64	3	2.0	9.3

材料：

糙米飯 ………… 720公克
高麗菜葉…4片(250公克)
肉丁 ……………… 80公克
洋葱末 …………… 50公克
麵粉 ……………… 2大匙

① {
太白粉、塩各¼小匙
胡椒粉 ……… ⅛小匙
}

② {
高湯 ………… 4杯
番茄醬 ……… ½杯
塩 ………… ¼小匙
胡椒粉 ……… ⅛小匙
}

❶ 將糙米飯、肉丁、洋葱末拌勻，再調入①料後，分成四份餡。

❷ 高麗菜葉4片入滾水中煮軟，取出，去硬梗部份(圖1)。

❸ 攤開高麗菜葉並擦乾水份，撒上麵粉(圖2)，包1份餡，用牙籤固定。

❹ 鍋裏排上高麗菜捲，加②料煮滾後，改小火熬至湯汁略收乾即盛起，餘汁留用，食時拔掉牙籤，淋上煮汁即成。

INGREDIENTS:

720g (25 oz)	Cooked Brown Rice
4 sheets (250g/8½ oz)	Cabbage Leaves
80g (2¾ oz)	Diced Pork
50g (1¾ oz)	Chopped Onions
2 T.	Flour

① {
¼ t. each: Cornstarch, Salt
⅛ t. Pepper
}

② {
4 c. Soup Stock
½ c. Ketchup
¼ t. Salt
⅛ t. Pepper
}

❶ To make filling, mix rice with diced pork and chopped onions; stir in ① and mix. Divide filling into 4 equal portions.

❷ Parboil cabbage leaves until soft. Trim off hard stems if any (Illust. ①).

❸ Spread out cabbage leaves and pat dry. Sprinkle each sheet with flour (Illust. ②). Place a portion of filling onto each sheet of cabbage, tuck in both ends and roll. Stablize with toothpicks.

❹ Arrange cabbage rolls in wok or skillet and add ②. Bring to boiling, reduce heat and simmer until only a little liquid remains. Remove rolls from wok and retain sauce. Arrange rolls on serving plate. Prior to serving, remove toothpicks and sprinkle on remaining sauce.

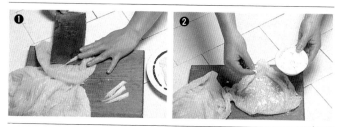

項目 Item 材料 Material	份量，重量 (公克) Unit/Wt. (g)	熱 量 (卡) Energy (Cal.)	蛋白質 (公克) Prot. (g)	脂 肪 (公克) Fat (g)	醣 類 (公克) CHO (g)
糙米飯 Cooked Brown Rice	720	1224	24.12	7.2	271.4
高麗菜葉 Cabbage Leaves	250	42.5	4.75	0.25	7.75
肉丁 Diced Pork	80	277.6	11.68	25.28	—
洋葱 Chopped Onion	50	12.5	0.45	0.2	2.5
番茄醬 Ketchup	120	111.6	1.92	0.36	28.2
合 計 Total		1668	42.9	33.3	310
一人份 Per Serving		278	7.2	5.5	51.6

黄豆糙米飯　Brown Rice with Soy Beans

材料：
黃豆（圖1）⋯⋯⋯⋯⋯ 半杯（80公克）
糙米（圖2）⋯⋯⋯⋯⋯ 2杯（400公克）
水⋯⋯⋯⋯⋯⋯⋯⋯⋯⋯⋯⋯ 2杯

❶ 黃豆洗淨，加水浸泡4小時，備用。
❷ 糙米洗淨，加泡好的黃豆及水2杯，放入電鍋內，外鍋加水3杯，煮至熟即可。

INGREDIENTS:

½ c. (80g/2¾ oz)　Soy Beans (Illust. ①)
2 c. (400g/14 oz)　Brown Rice (Illust. ②)
2 c. Water

❶ Rinse soy beans; add water and soak for 4 hours. Drain and set aside.
❷ Rinse brown rice and mix with pre-soaked soy beans; add 2 c. water and place into rice steamer. Pour 3 c. water into outer layer of steamer. Steam until cooked.

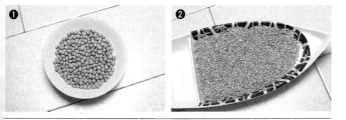

❶　❷

材料 Material	項目 Item 份量，重量 （公克） Unit/Wt. (g)	熱 量 （卡） Energy (Cal.)	蛋白質 （公克） Prot. (g)	脂 肪 （公克） Fat (g)	醣 類 （公克） CHO (g)
黃豆 Soybeans	80	260	29.44	14.4	22.16
糙米 Brown Rice	2 杯 PC. 400	1360	26.8	8	301.6
合 計 Total		1620	56.2	22.4	323.8
一人份 Per Serving		270	9.4	3.7	54

紅豆飯　Rice with Red Beans

材料：
紅豆(圖1)⋯⋯⋯⋯⋯⋯⋯⋯⋯ 60公克
白米⋯⋯⋯⋯⋯⋯⋯⋯1½杯(300公克)
糯米(圖2)⋯⋯⋯⋯⋯⋯½杯(100公克)
水⋯⋯⋯⋯⋯⋯⋯⋯⋯⋯⋯⋯ 8杯

❶紅豆洗淨，加1杯水泡隔夜，備用。
❷白米、糯米洗淨，加水2杯浸泡2小時備用。
❸將紅豆及1杯水放入電鍋之內鍋中，外鍋加5杯水，煮
　至熟(約2½小時)，瀝乾水份，備用。
❹將紅豆加入上述已浸泡之❷料中，外鍋放½杯水，用
　電鍋煮至熟，即成。

INGREDIENTS:

60g (2 oz)	Red Beans (Illust. ①)
1½ c. (300g/10½ oz)	White Rice
½ c. (100g/3½ oz)	Glutinous Rice (Illust. ②)
8 c.	Water

❶ Rinse red beans; add 1 c. water and soak over night. Without draining, place into inner layer of rice-cooker; Pour 5 c. water into outer layer. Steam until cooked (about 2½ hours). Remove, drain and set aside.

❷ Rinse both white and glutinous rice; add 2 c. water and soak for 2 hours without draining; add pre-steamed red beans, and place into inside layer of rice-cooker. Pour ½ c. water into outer layer of rice steamer and steam until done.

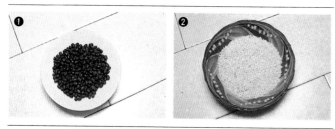

材料 Material	項目 Item 份量，重量 (公克) Unit/Wt. (g)	熱　量 (卡) Energy (Cal.)	蛋白質 (公克) Prot. (g)	脂　肪 (公克) Fat (g)	醣　類 (公克) CHO (g)
紅豆 Red Beans	60	186	12.78	0.42	33.96
白米 White Rice	1½ 杯C. 300	1062	9.5	1.5	234.3
糯米 Glutinous Rice	½ 杯C. 100	354	6.5	1.2	76.8
合　計 Total		1602	28.78	3.12	345
一人份 Per Serving		267	4.79	0.52	57.5

材料：

冬瓜	600公克
鷄腿	1隻(約260公克)
火腿	6片(約40公克)
冬菇	3朶(約6公克)
干貝(乾)	9公克
玻璃紙	1張

①
水	2杯
葱段	8段
薑片	2片
酒	½大匙
塩	½小匙
味精	¼小匙
胡椒粉	⅛小匙

❶冬菇泡軟，去蒂切半，干貝泡水備用。
❷冬瓜去皮以挖球器挖成球狀(圖1)，鷄腿切塊，以熱水川燙撈起。
❸將所有材料及①料同置燉盅內，用玻璃紙封口(圖2)，放進蒸鍋內蒸約40分鐘即成。

INGREDIENTS:

600g (1 lb. 5 oz)	Winter Squash
1 (260g/9 oz)	Chicken Leg
6 slices (40g/1⅖ oz)	Chinese or Virginia Ham
3 (6g)	Dried Black Mushrooms
9g	Dried Scallops
1 sheet	Cellophane or Heat-Proof Saran Wrap

①
2 c.	Water
8 segments	Green Onion
2 slices	Ginger
½ T.	Cooking Wine
½ t.	Salt
⅛ t.	Pepper

❶ Soak mushrooms until soft and trim off stems. Soak dried scallops in hot water for ½ hour; remove and drain.
❷ Pare winter squash and scoop into balls (Illust. ①). Chop chicken leg into bite-size pieces and scald in boiling water; remove and set aside.
❸ Place all ingredients in an earthenware pot or casserole. Mix in ① and cover with cellophane or saran wrap (Illust. ②). Place in steamer and steam for 40 minutes.

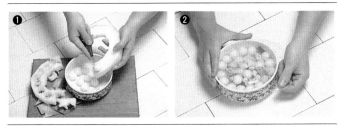

材料 Material \ 項目 Item	份量,重量 (公克) Unit/Wt. (g)	熱量 (卡) Energy (Cal.)	蛋白質 (公克) Prot. (g)	脂肪 (公克) Fat (g)	醣類 (公克) CHO (g)
冬瓜 Winter Squash	600	42	2.4	0.6	8.4
鷄腿 Chicken Leg	260	156	26.26	4.94	—
火腿 Chinese or Virginia Ham	40	209.6	7.6	19.6	0.08
冬菇 Dried Black Mushrooms	6	7.74	0.78	0.10	3.54
干貝 Dried Scallop	9	28.26	5.55	0.18	0.7
合計 Total		444	42.6	25.4	12.7
一人份 Per Serving		74	7.1	4.2	2.1

材料：

小排骨‧‧‧‧‧‧‧‧‧‧‧‧‧‧‧‧‧‧‧‧‧‧‧‧‧75公克
黃豆芽‧‧‧‧‧‧‧‧‧‧‧‧‧‧‧‧‧‧‧‧‧‧‧110公克
番茄(小)‧‧‧‧‧‧‧‧‧‧‧‧‧‧1個(約110公克)
油‧‧‧‧‧‧‧‧‧‧‧‧‧‧‧‧‧‧‧‧‧‧‧‧‧‧‧‧‧‧‧‧2大匙
① { 水‧‧‧‧‧‧‧‧‧‧‧‧‧‧‧‧‧‧‧‧‧‧‧‧‧‧‧9杯
　　薑‧‧‧‧‧‧‧‧‧‧‧‧‧‧‧‧‧‧‧‧‧‧‧‧‧‧‧2片
② { 塩‧‧‧‧‧‧‧‧‧‧‧‧‧‧‧‧‧‧‧‧‧‧‧‧‧‧2小匙
　　味精‧‧‧‧‧‧‧‧‧‧‧‧‧‧‧‧‧‧‧‧‧‧‧1小匙

❶排骨切小塊川燙撈起，番茄去皮(圖1、2)去籽，切丁備用。

❷鍋燒熱入油2大匙，將番茄略炒盛起。

❸排骨入①料燒開，改用小火煮40分鐘後，再下黃豆芽、番茄及②料續煮20分鐘即可。

INGREDIENTS:

75g (2⅔ oz)	Pork Ribs
110g (3¾ oz)	Soy Bean Sprouts
1 (110g/3½ oz)	Small Tomato
2 T.	Cooking Oil
① { 9 c.	Water
2 slices	Ginger
② 2 t.	Salt

❶ Chop ribs into bite-size pieces. Parboil, remove and drain. Peel tomato and remove seeds (Illust. ①, ②); dice and set aside.

❷ Heat wok and add 2 T. oil. Quickly stir-fry diced tomato and remove.

❸ Place ribs into pot with ① and bring to a boil. Reduce heat and simmer for 40 minutes. Add bean sprouts, pre-fried diced tomato and ②. Continue to simmer over low heat for 20 minutes.

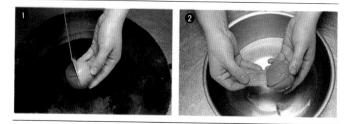

項目 Item / 材料 Material	份量，重量（公克）Unit/Wt. (g)	熱量（卡）Energy (Cal.)	蛋白質（公克）Prot. (g)	脂肪（公克）Fat (g)	醣類（公克）CHO (g)
黃豆芽 Soy Bean Sprouts	225	162	9	—	31.5
小排骨 Pork Back Ribs	150	672	20.18	64.8	—
番茄 Tomato	1 個 PC. 110	19.8	0.77	0.33	3.85
油 Cooking Oil	2 大匙 T. 30	270	0	30	0
合計 Total		1124	30	95.1	35.4
一人份 Per Serving		187	5	15.9	5.9

蔬菜濃湯 Vegetable Chowder

材料：

洋葱丁	150公克		油	1大匙
高麗菜	100公克		高湯	6杯
馬鈴薯丁	100公克	①	塩	2小匙
胡蘿蔔丁	100公克		味精	1小匙
番茄(小1個)	100公克			

❶高麗菜切塊備用，番茄川燙後，去皮去籽，切成丁狀。
❷鍋熱入油1大匙，炒香洋葱再入馬鈴薯丁、胡蘿蔔丁、
　高麗菜拌炒一下，再入①料，待滾後再下番茄丁煮約
　30分鐘即成。

INGREDIENTS:

150g (5¼ oz)	Chopped Onions
100g (3½ oz)	Cabbage
100g (3½ oz)	Diced Potatoes
100g (3½ oz)	Diced Carrots
100g (3½ oz)	Tomatoes
1 T.	Cooking Oil
① 6 c.	Soup Stock
2 t.	Salt

❶ Wash cabbage and cut into bite-size pieces. Scald tomatoes in boiling water; peel, remove seeds and dice.

❷ Heat wok, add 1 T. oil and stir-fry onions until fragrant. Mix in potatoes, carrots and cabbage. Continue to stir-fry. Add ① and bring to a boil. Then mix in diced tomatoes, reduce heat and simmer for 30 minutes.

材料 Material	份量，重量 （公克） Unit/Wt. (g)	熱 量 （卡） Energy (Cal.)	蛋白質 （公克） Prot. (g)	脂 肪 （公克） Fat (g)	醣 類 （公克） CHO (g)
洋葱丁 Chopped Onions	150	37.5	1.35	0.6	7.5
高麗菜 Cabbage	100	17	1.9	0.1	3.1
馬鈴薯 Diced Potatoes	100	75	2.3	0.1	16.9
胡蘿蔔 Diced Carrots	100	37	1.0	0.4	8.0
番茄 Tomato	100	18	0.7	0.3	3.5
油 Cooking Oil	1大匙 T. 15	135	0	15	0
合 計 Total		320	7.25	16.5	39
一人份 Per Serving		53	1.2	2.75	6.5

四色清湯 Four-Colored Consommé

材料：

小排骨	⋯⋯⋯⋯⋯⋯⋯	6塊（300公克）
水	⋯⋯⋯⋯⋯⋯⋯	8杯
塩	⋯⋯⋯⋯⋯⋯⋯	1小匙
①	筍絲⋯⋯⋯⋯⋯⋯	100公克
	木耳絲⋯⋯⋯⋯⋯	60公克
	香菇絲⋯⋯⋯⋯⋯	40公克
	金針⋯⋯⋯⋯⋯⋯	20公克

❶小排骨加水先以大火煮滾後，再以小火熬半小時即為高湯。

❷將①料及4杯的高湯入燉盅內，以蒸鍋蒸40分鐘即可。

INGREDIENTS:

6 pcs. (300g/10½ oz)	Pork Ribs
8 c.	Water
1 t.	Salt
① 100g (3½ oz)	Shredded Bamboo Shoots
60g (2 oz)	Shredded Dried Fungus (Black Wood Ear) (Illust. ①)
40g (1⅓ oz)	Shredded Dried Black Mushrooms
20g (¾ oz)	Dried Tiger Lily (Illust. ②)

❶ To make stock: Place ribs in pot with 8 c. water and allow to boil. Reduce heat and simmer for ½ hour.

❷ Place all ingredients in ① into casserole, with 4 c. stock from Step ❶. Place casserole in steamer and steam for 40 minutes.

材料 Material	項目 Item 份量，重量 （公克） Unit/Wt. (g)	熱 量 （卡） Energy (Cal.)	蛋白質 （公克） Prot. (g)	脂 肪 （公克） Fat (g)	醣 類 （公克） CHO (g)
筍絲 Shredded Bamboo Shoot	100	19	2.6	0.5	2.4
木耳 Shredded Dried Fungus	60	67.8	6.06	0.72	38.04
香菇 Shredded Dried Black Mushroom	40	51.6	5.2	0.68	23.6
金針 Dried Tiger Lily	20	50.8	1.7	0.5	11.9
小排骨 Pork Ribs	300	1344	40.35	129.6	—
合 計 Total		1533	55.9	132	75.9
一人份 Per Serving		256	9.3	22	12.7

豆腐青魚湯　Tuna Broth with Bean Curd

材料：

青魚肉	…………………………	220公克
豆腐	…………………	2塊（200公克）
葱花、薑絲	…………………	各1大匙
① 塩、酒	…………………	各⅛小匙

②
水	…………………………	5杯
塩	…………………………	¾小匙
糖	…………………………	½小匙
味精	…………………………	⅛小匙

❶魚肉切片（圖1）以①料略醃，豆腐切成12塊備用。
❷水燒開入豆腐川燙後撈起，置湯碗，將②料燒開入魚
　片（圖2）略煮即可倒入湯碗，撒上葱花、薑絲即成。

INGREDIENTS:

220g (7¾ oz)		Fresh Tuna Fillet
2	(200g/7 oz)	Bean Curd Squares
1 T.		Chopped Green Onions
1 T.		Shredded Ginger
①	⅛ t. each:	Salt, Cooking Wine
②	5 c.	Water
	¾ t.	Salt
	½ t.	Sugar

❶ Cut fish fillet(s) into thin slices (Illust. ①) and
marinate with ①. Cut bean curd squares into
12 small pieces.
❷ Scald bean curd pieces in boiling water, remove
and place in large soup bowl. Bring ② to boiling,
add fish slices (Illust. ②) and cook until done;
pour into soup bowl over bean curd; sprinkle
with chopped green onions and shredded ginger;
and serve immediately.

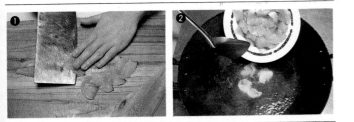

材料\項目 Material\Item	份量，重量 （公克） Unit/Wt. (g)	熱量 （卡） Energy (Cal.)	蛋白質 （公克） Prot. (g)	脂肪 （公克） Fat (g)	醣類 （公克） CHO (g)
青魚肉 Fresh Tuna Fillet	220	283.8	35.64	14.08	1.32
豆腐 Bean Curd Squares	2塊 PC. 200	130	12.8	8.4	3.6
糖 Sugar	½ 小匙 t. 2.5	10	—	—	2.5
合計 Total		424	48.4	22.5	7.4
一人份 Per Serving		71	8	3.8	1.2

糖尿病的飲食治療

　　糖尿病爲體內胰島素功能不足所引起之醣類代謝異常，使身體細胞對醣質的利用能力減低，造成血糖上升或尿糖發生，如此之新陳代謝障礙的慢性疾病亦會引發各種併發症，如視力喪失、尿毒症、血管硬化、神經麻痺等，若能早期注意飲食得當，病情可延緩惡化，故飲食控制對糖尿病患是很重要的。

　　糖尿病飲食治療目的在於供給足夠且均衡的營養，維持理想體重、避免血糖過高及避免或延遲併發症之發生，其飲食注意事項如下：

1. 切忌肥胖，保持理想體重。
2. 定時定量，每餐的飲食要依照計畫，不可任意增減。
3. 少吃油炸、油煎或油酥及豬皮、雞皮、鴨皮、魚皮等食物。
4. 花生、瓜子、腰果、核桃等含脂肪熱量較高的核果類亦應少吃。
5. 炒菜宜用植物油，忌用動物油。
6. 烹調方式多採用清蒸、水煮、涼拌、烤、燒、燴、燉、滷等。
7. 中老年人的飲食不可太鹹。
8. 少吃胆固醇含量高的食物，如：內臟、蟹黃、蝦卵、魚卵等。
9. 多選富含纖維質的食物，如全穀類的主食，未加工的豆類、蔬菜、水果，但不可超出計劃。
10. 含澱粉質高的食物，如：甘薯、馬鈴薯、芋頭、玉米、菱角、栗子、毛豆、乾豆類等，不可任意挑選食物，應按營養師指導食用。
11. 糖果、煉乳、汽水、罐裝果汁、蜜餞、蛋糕、中西甜鹹點心、冬粉、太白粉應儘量不吃。
12. 不吃加糖食物，嗜甜食者，可選用代糖代替糖調味。

Dietary Therapy for Diabetes

Diabetes is the abnormal metabolism of carbohydrates, caused by inadequate functioning of insulin in the body. As a result, the ability of body cells to use carbohydrates is decreased, which causes the increase in blood sugar or the occurrence of glycosuria. This chronic disease in ineffective metabolism may induce further complications, such as retinopathy, nephropathy, neuropathy, atherosclerosis, etc. If an appropriate diet is observed during the early stage, further impairment can be delayed substantially. It is therefore imperative that patients with diabetes adhere to a controlled dietary regimen.

The dietary therapy of diabetes aims at supplying adequate and balanced nutrition to maintain ideal body weight, preventing blood sugar level from escalating, and preventing or delaying the development of complications. Special attention should be paid to the following:

1. Do not become overweight. Attain and maintain an ideal body weight.
2. Take each meal as scheduled at fixed times, and in consistent amounts and distribution. Do not change the schedule.
3. Reduce the amount of foods prepared with deep-frying or pan-frying, and take only skinned pork, poultry and fish.
4. Nuts high in fat content, such as peanuts, seeds, cashew nuts, and walnuts, should be avoided.
5. Use vegetable oil (except coconut oil and palm oil) for cooking. Never cook in animal fat.
6. Cooking methods, such as steaming, boiling, braising, grilling, baking, broiling, stewing, etc., which need less fat, are recommended.
7. When preparing meals for the elderly, MSG and salt should be reduced.
8. Foods with high cholesterol content, such as organ meats, crab spawn, shrimp roe, fish roe, should be avoided.
9. Choose foods with higher fiber content, such as whole-grain cereals, unprocessed beans, fresh vegetables and fruits. However, do not consume in excess of prescribed amount.
10. Foods with high starch content, such as sweet potatoes, potatoes, taros, maizes, water-singharnuts, chestnuts, beans, dried beans, etc., should be taken only as advised by a dietician.
11. Candies, sweetened milk, soft drinks, canned fruit juices, preserved candied fruits, cakes, desserts, dim sum, bean thread, and pure starch should be avoided.
12. Do not eat sweetened foods. Saccharin may be substituted for sugar.

Frances C. Ma

舉例：一個女性糖尿病患，年齡56歲，身高155公分，體重55公斤，輕度工作者，則她可根據以下的表格換算出自己所需要的熱量。

糖尿病患理想的身高體重換算表

項目 年齡	身高(公分) 男	身高(公分) 女	體重(公斤) 男	體重(公斤) 女	
35歲↓	170	158	62	52	男身高若增減1公分 則體重增減0.6公斤
35-55歲	166	154	62	52	女身高若增減1公分 則體重增減0.5公斤
55歲↑	164	152	62	52	

糖尿病患熱量與體重的關係

所需熱量 分類	卡／公斤	卡／磅
減重者	20	9
臥床病人	25	11
輕度工作者	30	14
中度工作者	35	16
重度工作者	40	18

糖尿病患熱量的分配

項目 營養素	熱量百分比	每克所產生的熱量 (卡/公克)
醣　類	50%	4
脂　肪	30%	9
蛋白質	20%	4

根據以上表格得出以下結果：

155公分－152公分＝3公分──這位女性比理想身高高3公分
52公斤＋(0.5公斤×3)＝53.5公斤──這位女性的理想體重
30卡/公斤×53.5公斤＝1605卡──這位女性一天所需熱量
1605卡×50%÷4卡/公克＝200公克──醣類
1605卡×30%÷9卡/公克＝53.5公克──脂肪
1605卡×20%÷4卡/公克＝80公克──蛋白質

根據以上結果作成一份飲食分配表如下：

營養素 食物類別	份量 (X)	蛋白質 (公克)	脂肪 (公克)	醣類 (公克)	熱量 (卡)	早餐	午餐	晚餐	夜點
牛　奶(脫脂)	1	8	—	12	80				1
蛋	1	7	5	—	73	1			
蔬菜甲	2	—	—	—	—	1	½	½	
蔬菜乙	1	2		5	28		½	½	
肉　類	5	35	25	—	365	1	2	2	
豆製品	1	7	5		73		½	½	
水　果	2			20	80		1	1	
主食類	11	22	—	165	748	3	3½	3½	1
油	4		20	—	180	1	1½	1½	
合　計		81	55	202	1627				

由上表可知這位女性糖尿病患，每天所需熱量1605卡(包括醣類200公克、脂肪53.5公克、蛋白質80公克)，因此這位女性糖尿病患每天可食用的食物份量為：

牛奶(脫脂)1杯
蛋1個
蔬菜甲2份(每份100公克)
蔬菜乙1份(每份50公克)
肉類5份(每份平均約1兩，37.5公克)

豆製品1份(每份如豆腐1塊，100公克)
水果2份(如橘子100公克，約1份)
主食類11份(土司一片，乾飯¼碗為1份)
油4小匙

所以依上述的份量，設計這位糖尿病患一天三餐及夜點的菜單如下：(菜單取樣自本食譜的示範)

早餐：
三色蛋(見88頁) 1份
紅燒筍(見85頁) 1份
涼拌蝦仁(見74頁) 1份
稀飯1½碗

午餐：
釀番茄(見69頁) 1份
牛蒡牛肉絲(見71頁) 1份
涼拌双絲(見67頁) 1份
東江豆腐湯(見90頁) 1份
柳丁1個
飯七分滿

晚餐：
豆瓣魚(見75頁) 1份
涼拌干絲(見80頁) 1份
素菜捲(見82頁) 1份
羅宋湯(見92頁) 1份
飯七分滿
西瓜1片(250公克)

夜點：
脫脂奶 1杯(240c.c.)
土司 1片

A Guide to Designing Meals for the Diabetic Patient

Example: A female diabetic patient, aged 56, 155 cm. tall, weighing 55 kgs, engaged in light activity, may calculate her caloric requirements using the following figures:

Optimum height/weight for the diabetic patient:

Age \ Description	Height (cm) Male	Height (cm) Female	Weight (kg) Male	Weight (kg) Female	
35 or less	170	158	62	52	•Male: When 1 cm. taller/shorter, add/substract 0.6 kg. for weight.
35-55	166	154	62	52	•Female: when 1 cm. taller/shorter, add/substract 0.5 kg. for weight.
55 or more	164	152	62	52	

Caloric requirements per day in relation to weight/activity of diabetic patients:

Descriptions \ Energy	Calories/kg	Calories/lb
Overweight	20	9
Bedridden	25	11
Light activity	30	14
Moderate activity	35	16
Marked activity	40	18

Caloric distribution for the diabetic patient:

Nutrition \ Items	Calory percentages	Energy produced from each (calories/g)
Carbohydrates	50%	4
Fat	30%	9
Protein	20%	4

Based upon the figures above, we arrive at the following:
155cm – 152cm = 3cm — This woman is 3 cm taller than optimum height
52kg + (0.5kg × 3) = 53.5kg — Optimum weight for the woman
30 calories/kg × 53.5kg = 1,605 calories — Calories required/day
1,605 calories × 50% ÷ 4 calories/g = 200g — Carbohydrates
1,605 calories × 30% ÷ 9 calories/g = 53.5— Fat
1,605 calories × 20% ÷ 4 calories/g = 80g — Protein

Based upon the results above, a diet chart is formulated:

Nutrition	Quantity X	Prot. g.	Fat g.	CHO g.	Energy cal	Breakfast	Lunch	Supper	Snack
Skim milk	1	8	—	12	80				1
Egg	1	7	5	—	73	1			
Vegetables A	2	—	—	—	—	1	½	½	
Vegetables B	1	2	—	5	28		½	½	
Meat	5	35	25	—	365	1	2	2	
Bean products	1	7	5	—	73		½	½	
Fruits	2	—	—	20	80		1	1	
Staple foods	11	22	—	165	748	3	3½	3½	1
Oil	4	—	20	—	180	1	1½	1½	
Total		81	55	202	1627				

The figures above indicate that this woman requires 1,605 calories per day (inclusive of 200 grams from carbohydrates, 53.5 grams from fat, 80 grams from protein). The dietary plan for this woman, will therefore consist of:

Skim milk   1 cup
Egg   1
Vegetable A 2 portions (100 grams each)
Vegetable B 1 portion (50 grams)
Meat   5 portions (@37.5 grams)

Bean products 1 portion (e.g. 100g. of beancurd)
Fruits   2 portions (e.g. 100 grams orange)
Staple foods   11 portions (e.g. a slice of toast, ¼ bowl of rice per portion).
Oil   4t

In compliance with the requirements specified above for this woman, three meals and a bedtime snack have been designed as follows: (Specimens from Wei-Chuan Recipes)

Breakfast:
Tri-Colored Eggs (p. 88)   1 portion
Saucy Bamboo Shoots (p. 85)   1 portion
Shrimp Salad (p. 74)   1 portion
Congee   1½ bowls

Lunch:
Stuffed Tomatoes (p. 69)   1 portion
Stir-Fried Beef with Burdock (p. 71)   1 portion
Chicken and Bean Sprout Salad (p. 67)   1 portion
Stuffed Bean Curd Soup (p. 90)   1 portion
Orange   1
Rice   70% of a bowl.

Supper:
Braised Whole Fish with Hot Bean Paste (p. 75)   1 portion
Bean Curd Noodle and Celery Salad (p. 80)   1 portion
Vegetable Rolls (p. 82)   1 portion
Russian Borscht (p. 92)   1 portion
Rice   70% of a bowl
Watermelon   1 piece (250 g)

Bedtime Snack:
Skim milk   1 cup (240 cc)
Toast   1 slice

材料：

棒腿(小鷄腿去皮)‥‥‥‥3隻(約300公克)
豆豉‥‥‥‥‥‥‥‥‥‥‥1大匙(10公克)
蒜末、葱末、薑末‥‥‥‥‥‥ 各2小匙
① 醬油‥‥‥‥‥‥‥‥‥‥‥‥1½大匙
   酒‥‥‥‥‥‥‥‥‥‥‥‥‥‥1小匙
   胡椒粉、味精‥‥‥‥‥‥‥各⅛小匙
② 葱花‥‥‥‥‥‥‥‥‥‥‥‥1大匙
   紅辣椒末‥‥‥‥‥‥‥‥‥‥½小匙

❶棒腿洗淨，切成6塊，拌入豆豉、蒜末、葱末、薑末及
　①料，醃約半小時備用。
❷在電鍋外鍋放2½杯水，再放入醃好之棒腿蒸至爛(約
　需1小時左右)，食前灑上②料即成。
■棒腿去皮、去骨可食部份淨重爲225公克。

INGREDIENTS:

300g (10½ oz)   Skinned Chicken Legs
1 T. (10g/⅓ oz)   Fermented Black Beans
2 t. each: Minced Garlic, Scallion, Ginger
① { 1½ T.   Soysauce
   { 1 t.   Cooking Wine
   { ⅛ t.   Pepper
② { 1 T.   Chopped Green Onion
   { ½ t.   Chopped Red Pepper

❶ Clean chicken legs and chop into square
   (approx. 3 cm³ each). Mix with minced garlic
   scallion and ginger, and marinate with ① fo
   ½ hour.
❷ Pour 2½ c. water into outer layer of rice-cooker
   place marinated chicken in container and steam
   until tender (approx. 1 hour). Garnish with ②
   prior to serving.
■ Other steaming methods may be used, in which
   case the chicken should be placed on a heat
   resistant dish and steamed over high heat until
   tender (approx. 1 hour).
■ Chicken Legs — Net weight after removal of skin
   and bones. Calculation of measurements used
   in table are based on the E.P. method (edible
   portion only).

材料 Material	項目 Item	份量，重量 (公克) Unit/Wt. (g)	熱 量 (卡) Energy (Cal.)	蛋白質 (公克) Prot. (g)	脂 肪 (公克) Fat (g)	醣 類 (公克) CHO (g)
棒腿(去皮) Skinned Chicken Legs		225	382.5	70.88	6.75	—
豆豉 Fermented Black Beans	1 大匙 T.　10	17.8	1.94	1.1	0.46	
合 計 Total			400	72.8	7.9	0.5
一人份 Per Serving			67	12	1.3	0.1

材料：

鷄胸肉⋯⋯⋯⋯	110公克
金茸(圖1)⋯⋯⋯	250公克
茼蒿⋯⋯⋯⋯⋯	400公克
薑絲⋯⋯⋯⋯⋯	1大匙
油⋯⋯⋯⋯⋯⋯	1大匙

① 塩、味精⋯各⅛小匙
② 水⋯⋯⋯⋯⋯½杯
酒、麻油⋯各½小匙
塩⋯⋯⋯⋯⋯⅜小匙
味精⋯⋯⋯⋯⅛小匙

❶茼蒿去蒂及老葉（處理後淨重約300公克）洗淨，入滾水中川燙至熟，撈出，加①料拌勻，置大圓盤中，圍邊備用。

❷鷄胸肉切絲，金茸去尾部(圖2)（淨重約220公克），從中間切段，洗淨備用

❸鍋熱入油1大匙，爆香薑絲，續入鷄絲炒至熟，撈出備用。

❹鍋熱入金茸及②料，以中火煮至熟，續入已炒熟的鷄絲拌勻起鍋，放入大圓盤中心即成。

■麻油可依個人喜好添加，只是份量以½小匙爲限，以免攝取過多的油脂。

■重量採可食部份之淨重。

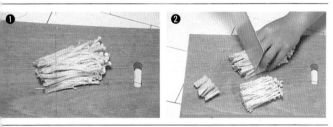

INGREDIENTS:

110g (4 oz)	Chicken Breast
250g (8¾ oz)	Golden Mushrooms (Illust. ①)
400g (14 oz)	Chinese Green Cabbage (Bok Choy)
1 T	Shredded Ginger
1 T	Cooking Oil

① ⅛ t. each: Salt
② ½ c. Water
½ t. each: Cooking Wine, Sesame Oil
⅜ t. Salt

❶ Wash bok choy; discard roots and any wilted leaves (net weight approx. 300g). Plunge into boiling water and cook till slightly done. Drain and remove. Mix with ①. Place on border of round platter.

❷ Cut chicken breast(s) into thin slices. Wash golden mushrooms and discard roots (net weight approx. 220g); cut in half (Illust. ②).

❸ Heat wok add 1 T. oil; stir-fry shredded ginger until fragrant. Add shredded chicken into wok and stir-fry until done. Remove and set aside.

❹ Re-heat wok and stir-fry golden mushrooms together with ② until done. Immediately add pre-cooked chicken and mix rapidly. Remove and place in center of platter.

■ Sesame oil may be added according to preference. However, in order to minimize fat consumption, no more than ½ t. should be used.

■ Calculation of measurements used in table are based on the E.P. method.

項目 Item 材料 Material	份量，重量 （公克） Unit/Wt. (g)	熱量 （卡） Energy (Cal.)	蛋白質 （公克） Prot. (g)	脂肪 （公克） Fat (g)	醣類 （公克） CHO (g)
茼蒿 Bok Choy	300	36	4.8	0.3	6.0
鷄胸肉 Chicken Breast	110	187	34.6	3.3	—
金茸 Golden Mushrooms	220	—	—	—	—
油 Cooking Oil	1 大匙 T. 15	135	0	15	0
麻油 Sesame Oil	½ 小匙 t. 2.5	22.5	0	2.5	0
合 計 Total		380	82.6	21.1	6
一人份 Per Serving		63	13.8	3.5	1

材料：

鷄胸肉‥‥‥‥‥ 220公克
番茄(紅)‥‥‥‥ 500公克
豌豆仁‥‥‥‥‥‥20公克
蛋白‥‥‥‥‥‥‥ 2個
油‥‥‥‥‥‥‥‥ 1大匙

①{
水‥‥‥‥‥ 2大匙
太白粉‥‥‥‥ 1小匙
塩‥‥‥‥‥‥3/8小匙
味精、胡椒粉‥‥‥‥
‥‥‥‥各1/8小匙
}

②{
水‥‥‥‥‥‥‥ 1杯
塩‥‥‥‥‥‥ 1小匙
酒、麻油‥‥各1/2小匙
味精‥‥‥‥‥‥1/8小匙
}

❶將鷄胸肉切細絲，入①料拌勻醃約30分鐘，入滾水川
燙至熟(約20秒)撈出備用。

❷將番茄洗淨去蒂，入滾水川燙(約10秒)撈出，去皮、
去籽(淨重300公克)，切成細丁備用。

❸鍋熱入油1大匙，將番茄拌炒數下，入②料煮至滾，再
入已打散的蛋白及豌豆仁，最後將已燙熟之鷄絲放入
一起拌勻即可起鍋。

■豌豆仁含醣份，可當配菜，不宜多食用。

■番茄含維他命C145毫克，重量爲可食部份之淨重。

INGREDIENTS:

220g (8 oz)	Chicken Breast
500g (1 lb 1½ oz)	Ripe Tomatoes
20g (⅔ oz)	Snow Peas
60g (2 oz)	Egg Whites
1 T.	Cooking Oil
① 2 T.	Water
1 t.	Cornstarch
⅜ t.	Salt
⅛ t.	Pepper
② 1 c.	Water
1 t.	Salt
½ t. each:	Cooking Wine, Sesame Oil

❶ Shred chicken breast(s) into thin strips and mix thoroughly with ①; marinate for 30 minutes. Blanch in boiling water until cooked (approx. 20 seconds). Drain and set aside.

❷ Wash tomatoes and discard stems and leaves. Scald in boiling water for approximately 10 seconds; drain. Remove skin and seeds; chop into small cubes.

❸ Heat wok then add 1 T. oil; add tomatoes and gently stir-fry; add ② and bring to boil. Beat egg whites and stir in. Immediately add snow peas and continue to stir-fry. Add pre-cooked shredded chicken and mix thoroughly.

■ Snow peas contain sugar and is therefore to be used sparingly.

■ Calculation of measurements used in table are based on the E.P. method.

項目 Item 材料 Material	份量，重量 (公克) Unit / Wt. (g)	熱 量 (卡) Energy (Cal.)	蛋白質 (公克) Prot. (g)	脂 肪 (公克) ·Fat (g)	醣 類 (公克) CHO (g)
鷄胸肉 Chicken Breast	220	374	69	6.6	—
番茄 Ripe Tomatoes	300	90	3.5	1.5	17.5
豌豆仁 Snow Peas	20	6.4	0.2	0.02	1.34
蛋白 Egg Whites	2 個 PC. 60	28.8	6.06	0.06	0.48
油 Cooking Oil	1 大匙 T. 15	135	0	15	0
麻油 Sesame Oil	½ 小匙 t. 2.5	22.5	0	2.5	0
合 計 Total		657	78.8	25.7	19.3
一人份 Per Serving		109	13.1	4.3	3.2

材料：

鷄胸肉…………… 110公克
豆芽……………… 300公克
韭菜(圖1)…………2枝
辣椒………………½條
水………………… 4杯
薑………………… 3片

① ┌塩…………³⁄₈小匙
　│麻油、酒…各½小匙
　│味精、胡椒粉………
　└…………各⅛小匙

❶水4杯燒滾，入鷄胸肉片及薑片，以小火煮至熟(約15分鐘)，撈出待涼，撕成絲狀，備用。
❷將豆芽去頭尾(處理後淨重約230公克)洗淨，韭菜也洗淨切段(圖2)(約20公克)，辣椒切絲備用。
❸將豆芽、韭菜入滾水川燙(約5秒)，撈出瀝乾，趁熱入①料及鷄絲拌匀，再灑上辣椒即成。

■重量採可食部份之淨重

INGREDIENTS:

110g (4 oz)	Chicken Breast
300g (10½ oz)	Green Bean Sprouts
20g (⅔ oz)	Leeks (cut into segments) (Illust. ①)
½	Red Pepper
4 c.	Water
3 slices	Ginger
① ⅜ t.	Salt
½ t. each:	Sesame Oil, Cooking Wine
⅛ t.	Pepper

❶ Boil 4 cups water; cook chicken breast(s) with 3 slices ginger over low heat until done (approx. 15 minutes). Drain and cool. Finger-shred chicken into thin slices and set aside.

❷ Wash bean sprouts; remove roots and tips (net weight approx. 230g) (Illust. ②). Slice red pepper into thin strips.

❸ Scald bean sprouts and leeks in boiling water for about 5 seconds. Drain. While still warm, add ① and mix thoroughly. Add shredded chicken and toss. Garnish with shredded red pepper and serve.

■ Calculation of measurements used in table are based on the E.P. method.

項目 Item 材料 Material	份量，重量 (公克) Unit／Wt. (g)	熱 量 (卡) Energy (Cal.)	蛋白質 (公克) Prot. (g)	脂 肪 (公克) Fat (g)	醣 類 (公克) CHO (g)
鷄胸肉 Chicken Breast	110	187	34.6	3.3	—
豆芽 Green Bean Sprouts	230	34.5	4.14	0.23	4.6
韭菜 Leeks	2 枝 PC. 20	3.4	0.44	0.08	0.88
油 Cooking Oil	½ 小匙 t. 2.5	22.5	—	2.5	—
合 計 Total		247	39.2	6.1	5.5
一人份 Per Serving		41	6.5	1.0	0.9

材料：

苦瓜⋯⋯⋯1條（450公克）
絞肉⋯⋯⋯⋯⋯⋯220公克

① { 水⋯⋯⋯⋯⋯4大匙
醬油⋯⋯⋯⋯⋯1小匙
塩⋯⋯⋯⋯⋯¼小匙
味精⋯⋯⋯⋯⅛小匙

② { 水⋯⋯⋯⋯⋯½杯
豆豉（洗過）⋯1大匙
紅辣椒末⋯⋯1小匙
塩⋯⋯⋯⋯⋯½小匙
味精⋯⋯⋯⋯少許

③ { 水⋯⋯⋯⋯⋯½小匙
太白粉⋯⋯⋯½小匙

❶苦瓜洗淨，整條切段（圖1），每段長約3公分，去籽（處理後淨重約350公克），入水煮3分鐘撈出備用。
❷絞肉與①料拌勻，甩打數次，分成6份，釀入苦瓜中（圖2），加②料大火蒸45分鐘後將蒸汁倒出以③料勾芡淋在苦瓜上即成。
■重量採可食部份之重量

INGREDIENTS:

450g (1 lb)	Bitter Gourd	
220g (8 oz)	Ground Pork	
①	{ 4 T.	Water
	1 t.	Soysauce
	¼ t.	Salt
②	{ ½ c.	Water
	1 T.	Fermented Black Beans (washed and drained)
	1 t.	Minced Red Pepper
	½ t.	Salt
③	{ ½ t.	Water } mix
	½ t.	Cornstarch

❶ Wash bitter gourd(s), cut off ends (Illust. ①) and slice at 3 cm. intervals. Remove seeds (net weigh approx. 350g). Cook in boiling water for 3 minutes Remove and drain.

❷ Season ground pork with ① and mix thoroughly Divide into 6 portions; stuff into hollows of bitte gourds (Illust. ②). Arrange on dish, add ② and steam over high heat for 45 minutes. When done pour out liquid into sauce pan and bring to boil. Stir in ③ to thicken; pour on stuffed bitte gourds and serve.

■ Calculation of measurements used in table are based on the E.P. method.

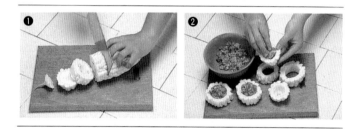

材料 Material	項目 Item	份量，重量 （公克） Unit/Wt.. (g)	熱　量 （卡） Energy (Cal.)	蛋白質 （公克） Prot. (g)	脂　肪 （公克） Fat (g)	醣　類 （公克） CHO (g)
苦瓜 Bitter Gourds		1 條 PC. 350	45.5	2.45	0.35	23.1
絞肉 Ground Pork		220	763.4	32.12	69.52	—
合　計 Total			808.9	34.6	69.9	23.1
一人份 Per Serving			134.8	5.8	11.7	3.9

釀 番 茄 Stuffed Tomatoes

材料：

紅番茄……3個（400公克）
絞肉（瘦）………150公克
蝦仁………………70公克
香菜………………少許

① 水…………… 6大匙
葱末、蒜末………
………………各1大匙
薑末…………½大匙
麻油…………½小匙
塩…………³⁄₈小匙
味精、胡椒粉………
…………各⅛小匙

❶紅番茄洗淨，去蒂對半切再去籽（圖1）（處理後淨重約250公克）。

❷蝦仁去腸泥洗淨切碎，加入絞肉及①料拌勻，分成6份釀入番茄內（圖2），正中央放一片香菜，大火蒸約10分鐘至熟即成。

■重量採可食部份之重量。

INGREDIENTS:

3 (400g/14 oz)	Ripe Tomatoes	
150g (5¼ oz)	Lean Ground Pork	
70g (2½ oz)	Raw Shelled Shrimp	
1-2 Sprigs	Coriander	

①
- 6 T. — Water
- 1 T. each: — Minced Green Onion, Minced Garlic
- ½ T. each: — Minced Ginger, Sesame Oil
- ³⁄₈ t. — Salt
- ⅛ t. — Pepper

❶ Wash tomatoes and discard stems. Cut each into half (Illust. ①) and remove seeds (net weight approx. 250g).

❷ Wash shrimp, devein and mince. Mix with ground pork and add ①; mix thoroughly. Divide into 6 portions and stuff into halved tomatoes (Illust. ②). Place 1 leaf of coriander at center of filling in each tomato half and steam over high heat until done (about 10 minutes).

■ Calculation of measurements used in table are based on the E.P. method.

材料 Material \ 項目 Item	份量，重量（公克）Unit/Wt. (g)	熱量（卡）Energy (Cal.)	蛋白質（公克）Prot. (g)	脂肪（公克）Fat (g)	醣類（公克）CHO (g)
紅番茄 Ripe Tomatoes	250	45	1.75	0.75	8.75
絞肉（瘦）Lean Ground Pork	150	520.5	21.9	47.4	—
蝦仁 Raw Shelled Shrimp	70	60.9	12.88	0.49	0.28
油 Cooking Oil	½ 小匙 t. 2.5	22.5	0	2.5	0
合計 Total		648.9	36.5	51.1	9.0
一人份 Per Serving		108.5	6.1	8.5	1.5

材料：

火鍋牛肉薄片···	220公克	水··············	3大匙
綠豆芽··········	150公克	塩、酒、麻油·	
洋葱··············	150公克 ①	··········	各½小匙
油··············	1大匙	黑胡椒·········	¼小匙
		味精··········	⅛小匙

❶綠豆芽去頭尾（處理後淨重約80公克）洗淨，洋葱切絲備用。

❷鍋熱入油2小匙，炒香洋葱，續入①料，以小火煮至洋葱變軟（約5分鐘），再加入已去頭尾的綠豆芽拌勻，即成內餡，分成12份備用。

❸將牛肉片分成12份，每一份牛肉片包1份餡（圖1），捲成圓筒狀（圖2）備用。

❹鍋燒熱入油1小匙，放入已捲好的牛肉捲煎至熟即可。

■洋葱富含醣份，不宜多食用。

■重量採可食部份之重量。

INGREDIENTS:

220g (8 oz)	Thinly Sliced Beef
150g (5¼ oz)	Green Bean Sprouts
150g (5¼ oz)	Onion
1 T.	Cooking Oil
① 3 T.	Water
½ t. each:	Salt, Cooking Wine, Sesame Oil
¼ t.	Black Pepper

❶ Remove tips and ends of bean sprouts (net weight approx. 80g); wash and drain. Slice onion into thin strips and set aside.

❷ Heat wok then add 2 t. oil; stir-fry onion strips until fragrant and season by adding all of ①. Simmer until onion tender (approx. 5 minutes). Add sprouts and mix thoroughly. This is the filling. Remove and divide into 12 portions.

❸ Divide beef slices into 12 portions. Wrap each portion of filling with a slice of beef, and roll into cylindrical shapes (Illust. ①).

❹ Heat wok and add 1 t. oil. Gently place rolls and sauté until done.

■ Onions contain large amounts of sugar, and consumption should therefore be monitored.

■ Calculation of measurements used in table are based on the E.P. method.

材料 Material	項目 Item 份量・重量 (公克) Unit/Wt. (g)	熱 量 (卡) Energy (Cal.)	蛋白質 (公克) Prot. (g)	脂 肪 (公克) Fat (g)	醣 類 (公克) CHO (g)
牛肉 Beef	220	292.6	41.36	12.76	—
綠豆芽 Bean Sprouts	80	12	1.44	0.08	1.6
洋葱 Onion	150	37.5	1.35	0.6	7.5
油 Cooking Oil	1 大匙 T. 15	135	0	15	0
麻油 Sesame Oil	1 小匙 t. 2.5	22.5	0	2.5	0
合 計 Total		499.6	44.2	30.9	9.1
一人份 Per Serving		83.3	7.4	5.2	1.5

材料：

牛肉…………… 110公克
牛蒡 ………………1根
（約200公克）
薑絲…………… 1大匙
油………………… 1大匙

① { 水……………¼杯
純釀醬油…… 1大匙
酒、麻油…各½小匙
味精………⅛小匙

② { 水………… 1大匙
太白粉………½小匙

❶將牛肉切細絲，牛蒡去皮(圖1)洗淨切段後，再切細絲(圖2)(淨重120公克)備用。

❷鍋熱入油1大匙，爆香薑絲，再入牛肉絲快炒至熟，撈出備用。

❸鍋熱入牛蒡及①料煮至熟，續加入炒熟的牛肉絲拌勻，最後以②料勾芡即成。

■牛蒡去皮切細絲後，必須浸在水中，以免顏色變黑。
■重量採可食部份之重量。

INGREDIENTS:

110g (4 oz)	Shredded Beef Fillet
200g (7 oz)	Burdock (Illust. ①)
1 T.	Shredded Ginger
1 T.	Cooking Oil

① { ¼ c. — Water
1 T. — Soysauce
½ t. each: — Cooking Wine, Sesame Oil

② { 1 T. — Water
½ t. — Cornstarch } mix

❶ Pare burdock and wash. Cut into segments and shred (Illust. ②) (net weight approx. 120g).

❷ Heat wok and add 1 T. oil. Stir-fry shredded ginger until fragrant; add shredded beef and continue to stir-fry until done. Remove and set aside.

❸ Re-heat wok and add burdock; mix in ① and stir-fry until done. Add pre-fried beef and mix thoroughly. Pour in mixture ② to thicken sauce.

■ To prevent discoloring of pared and shredded burdock, keep immersed in water. Drain prior to frying.

■ Calculation of measurements used in table are based on the E.P. method.

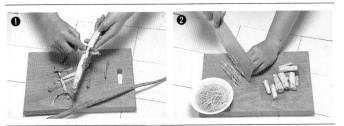

項目 Item / 材料 Material	份量，重量 (公克) I Unit/Wt. (g)		熱 量 (卡) Energy (Cal.)	蛋白質 (公克) Prot. (g)	脂 肪 (公克) Fat (g)	醣 類 (公克) CHO (g)
牛肉 Shredded Beef Fillet		110	146.3	20.68	6.38	—
牛蒡 Burdock		120	88.8	3.0	0.12	20.64
油 Cooking Oil	1 大匙 T.	15	135	0	15	0
太白粉 Cornstarch	½ 小匙 t.	2.5	8.43	0.03	0.01	2
麻油 Sesame Oil	½ 小匙 t.	2.5	22.5	0	2.5	0
合 計 Total			401.0	23.7	24.0	22.6
一人份 Per Serving			66.8	4.0	4.0	3.8

材料：

鱈魚	320公克	
海帶	240公克	
柴魚	20公克	
薑絲	2大匙	
水	6杯	

①
- 酒、麻油…各½小匙
- 塩…………¼小匙
- 味精…………⅛小匙
- 胡椒粉…………1/12小匙

②
- 酒、麻油…各½小匙
- 塩…………¼小匙
- 味精…………1/12小匙

❶將鱈魚洗淨去骨去皮（圖1）（處理後約220公克），切成6塊長方體（每塊約1×7×1公分）加①料醃半小時備用。

❷海帶切成六等份（每份約7×12公分）加柴魚及6杯水，以小火煮至爛（約1小時）撈出，餘汁過濾取½杯備用。

❸將每條海帶攤開，包入一塊魚及數根薑絲，捲好後以牙籤固定（圖2），置盤淋上海帶餘汁及②料以大火蒸至熟（約5分鐘）即成。

■重量採可食部份之重量

INGREDIENTS:

320g (11¼ oz)	Codfish
240g (8¼ oz)	Kelp
20g (¾ oz)	Shredded Dried Stock Fish
2 T.	Shredded Ginger
6 c.	Water

①
- ½ t. each: Cooking Wine, Sesame Oil
- ¼ t.: Salt
- 1/12 t.: Pepper

②
- ½ t. each: Cooking Wine, Sesame Oil
- ¼ t.: Salt

❶ Clean fish; remove skin and bones (Illust. ①) (net weight approx. 220g) and cut into 6 rectangular pieces (approx. 1x1x7cm). Add seasoning ① and marinate for ½ hour.

❷ Cut kelp into 6 equal portions (approx. 7x12cm) and cook in 6 cups water together with dried stock fish until tender (approx. 1 hour). Remove and drain. Strain soup and retain ½ cup for later use.

❸ Place 1 piece fish and a few strips of ginger onto each sheet of kelp. Wrap and roll; use toothpicks to stabilize (Illust. ②); arrange rolls on platter and sprinkle with retained kelp soup mixed with ②. Steam over high heat until cooked (approx. 5 minutes).

■ Calculation of measurements used in table are based on the E.P. method.

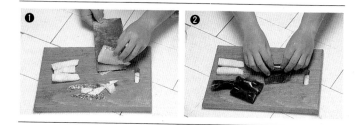

材料 Material	項目 Item	份量・重量 （公克） Unit/Wt. (g)	熱量 （卡） Energy (Cal.)	蛋白質 （公克） Prot. (g)	脂肪 （公克） Fat (g)	醣類 （公克） CHO (g)
鱈魚 Codfish		220	287	28.6	18.3	0.15
海帶 Kelp		240	55.2	2.4	0.48	12.72
油 Cooking Oil	1 小匙 t.	5	45	0	5.0	0
合 計 Total			387.2	31	23.78	12.9
一人份 Per Serving			64.5	5.2	3.9	2.2

清蒸白鯧 Steamed Pomfret

材料：
白鯧魚(1尾)……550公克
葱(切絲)…………… 2枝
薑(切絲)…………… 3片
油……………… 1大匙
紅辣椒(切絲)……… 1條

① 塩……………¾小匙
酒……………½小匙
胡椒粉、味精………
…………各⅛小匙

❶白鯧魚洗淨，以①料醃10～20分鐘再灑上葱絲、薑絲
及油1大匙，大火蒸約15分鐘，最後灑上紅辣椒絲即成。

■如果魚較小，蒸的時間必須縮短，可以用牙籤插看魚
肉，不沾牙籤即可。

INGREDIENTS:

1 (550g/1 lb 3½ oz)		Whole Pomfret
2 stalks		Shredded Green Onion
3 slices		Shredded Ginger
1		Shredded Red Pepper
1 T.		Cooking Oil
①	¾ t.	Salt
	½ t.	Cooking Wine
	⅛ t.	Pepper

❶ Scale and clean fish. Rub with ① and marinate for 10-20 minutes. Sprinkle green onion, ginger and 1 T. oil on top and steam over high heat for about 15 minutes. Garnish with shredded red pepper and serve.

■ Steaming time may be adjusted in accordance with size of fish. To test if done, poke with toothpick. Flesh will not stick to toothpick when fish is thoroughly cooked.

項目 Item 材料 Material	份量・重量 (公克) Unit/Wt. (g)	熱 量 (卡) Energy (Cal.)	蛋白質 (公克) Prot. (g)	脂 肪 (公克) Fat (g)	醣 類 (公克) CHO (g)
白鯧 Whole Pomfret	1 尾 PC. 550	242	53.9	1.1	1.1
油 Cooking Oil	1 大匙 T 15	135	0	15	0
合 計 Total		377	53.9	16.1	1.1
一人份 Per Serving		63	9.0	2.7	0.2

材料：
大蝦仁…………… 225公克
高麗菜……………50公克

① | 冷開水……… 3大匙
白醋……… 2½大匙
生薑汁…… 1½大匙
巴西利末、薑末……
各1大匙
塩………… ⅜小匙
代糖………… 1/12小匙

❶蝦仁去腸泥(圖1)，加少許塩洗淨，瀝乾水份，入滾水中燙熟撈出(圖2)，即刻漂冷水備用。

❷高麗菜洗淨切絲，放在盤中，再排上蝦仁，蓋上保鮮膜，放入冰箱。

❸食用前淋上①料，拌勻即可。

■1.涼拌蝦仁，最好選購新鮮帶殼的蝦，買回自己剝殼以確保新鮮度。

2.代糖之定義：是專為過重和糖尿病人而製造糖的代替品，不含葡萄糖，對糖尿病人而言，不會如一般純糖含葡萄糖，則使得血糖快速上升，而影響病情。

■重量採可食部份之重量。

INGREDIENTS:

225g (8 oz)　Large Raw Shelled Shrimp
50g (1¾ oz)　Cabbage

① | 3 T.　Water
2½ T.　White Vinegar
1½ T.　Ginger Juice
1 T. each:　Minced Ginger,
　　　　　Minced Parsley | Dressing
⅜ t.　Salt
1/12 t.　Sugar Substitute.

❶ Clean and devein shrimp (Illust. ①). Mix gently with a dash of salt and wash. Rinse and drain. Blanch in boiling water until cooked (Illust. ②). Swiftly remove, drain and immediately plunge into cold water. Remove, drain and set aside.

❷ Wash cabbage and shred. Place in center of serving plate. Add pre-cooked shrimp on top of cabbage and refrigerate. Combine all ingredients in ① to make dressing and sprinkle on shrimp prior to serving.

■ To ensure freshness of shrimp, it is advisable to purchase them in the shell.

■ Calculation of measurements used in table are based on the E.P. method.

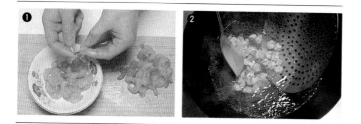

材料 Material	項目 Item	份量‧重量 （公克） Unit/Wt. (g)	熱　量 （卡） Energy (Cal.)	蛋白質 （公克） Prot. (g)	脂　肪 （公克） Fat (g)	醣　類 （公克） CHO (g)
蝦仁 Shelled Raw Shrimp		225	195.75	41.4	1.58	0.9
高麗菜 Cabbage		50	8.50	0.95	0.05	1.55
合　計 Total			204.3	42.4	1.6	2.5
一人份 Per Serving			34.1	7.1	0.3	0.4

豆瓣魚 Braised Whole Fish With Hot Bean Paste

材料：
吳郭魚(1尾)……600公克
油………………1小匙
① { 塩………………1小匙
     薑片……………6片

② { 水………………1杯
     葱末…………2大匙
     薑末、蒜末、豆瓣醬
     …………各1大匙
     醬油…………2小匙
     味精………¼小匙
     代糖………⅛小匙
③ 麻油、酒…各½小匙

❶魚洗淨，魚身兩面各劃二道斜刀，入①料醃1小時(中途必須將魚翻身)備用。
❷魚淋油1小匙，入蒸鍋蒸約10分鐘即熟，取出備用。
❸鍋熱入②料燒開，加③料後，即刻起鍋，淋於魚上即成。

INGREDIENTS:

600g (1 lb 5 oz)	Whole Fish
1 t.	Cooking Oil

① { 1 t.   Salt
    6 slices   Ginger

② { 1 c.   Water
    2 T.   Chopped Green Onion
    1 T. each: Chopped Ginger, Chopped
                Garlic, Hot Bean Paste
    2 t.   Soysauce
    ⅛ t.   Sugar Substitute

③ ½ t. each: Sesame Oil, Cooking Wine

❶ Scale and clean fish. Make a cut diagonally through the flesh on each side. Rub with ① and marinate for 1 hour, remembering to turn it over once.
❷ Sprinkle marinated fish with 1 t. oil and steam until thoroughly cooked (about 10 minutes).
❸ Heat wok, bring ② to a boil, and stir in ③. Immediately pour on fish and serve.

材料 Material	份量，重量 Unit/Wt. (公克) (g)	熱量 Energy (卡) (Cal.)	蛋白質 Prot. (公克) (g)	脂肪 Fat (公克) (g)	醣類 CHO (公克) (g)
吳郭魚 Whole Fish	1 尾 PC. 600	252	50.4	3.6	1.8
油 Cooking Oil	1 小匙 t. 5	45	0	5	0
豆瓣醬 Hot Bean Paste	1 大匙 T. 15	20.9	1.8	0.9	1.8
麻油 Sesame Oil	½ 小匙 t. 2.5	22.5	0	2.5	0
合計 Total		340	52.2	12	3.6
一人份 Per Serving		57	8.7	2	0.6

材料：

生魷魚	300公克	葱	2支	
筍片	50公克	薑	4片	
胡蘿蔔片	40公克	水	¾杯	
青椒	100公克	油	1大匙	
① { 塩	½小匙	② 酒、麻油…各½小匙		
味精	⅛小匙			

❶生魷魚除內臟洗淨，去薄膜，魷魚身切花（淨重 300
公克），青椒洗淨，去籽（淨重100公克）切塊，葱切段
均備用。

❷¾杯水燒開，入筍片、胡蘿蔔片，煮熟，續加青椒川燙
一下，即將所有材料起鍋備用。

❸鍋熱入油一大匙，爆香葱、薑，加生魷魚快炒，續加
❷ 步驟所有材料再以①料調味，最後入②料拌炒即成。

■在②料中可添加太白粉、水各½小匙，以增加滑嫩性
與光亮度，只是太白粉不宜任意使用，必須與米飯類
一齊代換，以免食用過量的醣份。

■重量採可食部份之重量。

INGREDIENTS:

300g (10½ oz)	Cuttlefish
50g (1¾ oz)	Sliced Bamboo Shoots
40g (1⅓ oz)	Sliced Carrot
100g (3½ oz)	Green Bell Pepper
2 stalks	Green Onion
4 slices	Ginger
¾ c.	Water
1 T.	Cooking Oil
① ½ t.	Salt

② ½ t. each: Cooking Wine, Sesame oil

❶ Cut off heads, tentacles, and tails of cuttlefish.
Peel off thin membrane from surface and remove
long transparent bone. Score inside surface both
lengthwise and across, and cut into bite-size
pieces. Wash green pepper, remove seeds and
cut into bite-size pieces. Set aside.

❷ Boil ¾ cup water and add bamboo shoots and
carrot slices. Cook until done. Scald green
pepper. Remove and drain.

❸ Cut green onion into segments. Heat wok, add
1 T. oil, and stir-fry green onion and ginger slices
until fragrant. Add cuttlefish and stir-fry briskly.
Add bamboo shoots, carrot and green pepper
(from step ❷), then mix in ①. Quickly stir in ②
and serve.

■ To enhance smoothness and brilliance, a mixture
of ½ t. cornstarch and ½ t. water may be added
to ②. However, consumption of cornstarch as
well as other carbohydrates should be closely
monitored by diabetics in order to control glucose
level.

■ Calculation of measurements used in table are
based on the E.P. method.

材料 Material	份量，重量 (公克) Unit/Wt. (g)		熱量 (卡) Energy (Cal.)	蛋白質 (公克) Prot. (g)	脂肪 (公克) Fat (g)	醣類 (公克) CHO (g)
魷魚 Cuttlefish	300		234	49.2	2.4	0.9
筍 Bamboo Shoots	50		10	1.75	0.05	1.8
胡蘿蔔 Carrot	40		14.8	0.4	0.16	3.2
青椒 Green Bell Pepper	100		16	1.0	0.2	3.3
油 Cooking Oil	1 大匙 T.	15	135	0	15	0
麻油 Sesame Oil	½ 小匙 t.	2.5	22.5	0	2.5	0
合計 Total			398.4	52.4	16.8	9.2
一人份 Per Serving			66.4	8.7	2.8	1.5

材料：

百頁	・・・・・・・・・・・	6张
蝦仁	・・・・・・・・・・	70公克
絞肉	・・・・・・・・・・	70公克
香菇	・・・・・・・・・・・・	2朵
熟筍絲	・・・・・・・・	30公克

① { 熱水 ・・・・・・・・・・ 2杯
    小蘇打 ・・・・・・ 1小匙

② { 葱末、薑末 各1小匙
    麻油・・・・・・・・・・½小匙
    味精、塩、酒・・・・・・・
    ・・・・・・・・・・ 各¼小匙
    胡椒粉・・・・・・・・⅛小匙

③ { 水・・・・・・・・・・・・½杯
    塩、太白粉各¼小匙
    味精・・・・・・・・・⅛小匙

❶將百頁以①料浸泡(圖1)20分鐘後，用清水沖洗多次備用。

❷蝦仁去腸泥，洗淨後切小丁，絞肉剁成泥狀，香菇泡軟去蒂切絲備用。

❸蝦仁丁、絞肉及②料拌勻成餡(圖2)後，分成6份，將每一片百頁包一份肉餡，捲成春捲狀置盤，再放入蒸鍋內，以大火蒸約10分鐘，取出備用。

❹香菇絲、熟筍絲及③料入鍋燒滾後，淋在百頁捲上即成。

■重量採可食部份之重量。

INGREDIENTS:

6 pcs.		Bean Curd Sheets
70g (2½ oz)		Raw Shelled Shrimp
70g (2½ oz)		Ground Pork
2		Dried Black Mushrooms
30g (1 oz)		Shredded Pre-cooked Bamboo Shoots

① { 2 c. — Hot Water
    1 t. — Baking Soda } mix

② { 1 t. each: — Minced Green Onion, Minced Ginger
    ½ t. — Sesame Oil
    ¼ t. each: — Salt, Cooking Wine
    ⅛ t. — Pepper

③ { ½ c. — Water
    ¼ t. each: — Salt, Cornstarch

❶ Soak bean curd sheets in mixture ① for 20 minutes (Illust. ①). Rinse several times with cold water to remove baking soda odor. Drain and set aside.

❷ Devein shrimp. Wash and chop finely until pasty. Soak mushrooms in warm water until soft, trim stems and shred.

❸ Blend ground pork and shrimp paste with ② to make stuffing (Illust. ②). Divide into 6 portions. Wrap a portion of stuffing into each sheet of bean curd and roll with ends tucked in. Arrange on heat-proof platter and steam over high heat for 10 minutes. Remove when ready.

❹ Mix shredded mushrooms and bamboo shoots with ③ and bring to a boil. Pour mixture over rolls and serve.

■ Calculation of measurements used in table are based on the E.P. method.

項目 Item / 材料 Material	份量，重量 (公克) Unit/Wt. (g)	熱 量 (卡) Energy (Cal.)	蛋白質 (公克) Prot. (g)	脂 肪 (公克) Fat (g)	醣 類 (公克) CHO (g)
百頁 Bean Curd Sheets	6 张 PC. 60	279.6	31.02	15.06	6.72
蝦仁 Raw Shelled Shimp	70	60.9	12.88	0.49	0.28
絞肉 Ground Pork	70	384.3	8.61	38.36	—
筍 Bamboo Shoots	30	5.7	0.78	0.15	0.72
油 Cooking Oil	½ 小匙 t. 2.5	22.5	0	2.5	0
合 計 Total		753	53.3	56.6	7.7
一人份 Per Serving		125.5	8.9	9.4	1.3

材料：

大白菜⋯⋯⋯⋯ 600公克
① 嫩豆腐(切塊)⋯ 1塊
　 胡蘿蔔(切片)30公克
　 筍(切片)⋯⋯⋯60公克
　 花菇⋯⋯⋯⋯⋯ 3朵
　 海帶捲(6捲)180公克
蒜苗(圖1)(切斜段)(圖2)
⋯⋯⋯⋯⋯⋯⋯⋯1枝

② 葱⋯⋯⋯⋯⋯⋯ 1枝
　 薑⋯⋯⋯⋯⋯⋯ 4片
③ 去油高湯⋯⋯⋯3杯
　 塩⋯⋯⋯⋯⋯½小匙
　 胡椒粉、味精
　 ⋯⋯⋯⋯各⅛小匙
油⋯⋯⋯⋯⋯⋯ 1大匙

❶大白菜洗淨切1.5公分粗條，燙軟備用，花菇泡軟對切備用。

❷砂鍋燒熱，入油1大匙，爆香②料後入③料煮開，先放已燙軟的大白菜再將①料排在上面，再次煮沸後改小火煮約20分鐘，灑上蒜苗即可上桌。

■重量採可食部份之重量。

INGREDIENTS:

600g (1 lb 5 oz)		Nappa Cabbage
①	1 square	Tender Bean Curd (cut into smaller pieces)
	30g (1 oz)	Carrot
	60g (2 oz)	Sliced Bamboo Shoots
	3	Dried Black Mushrooms
	180g (4⅘ oz)	Rolled Kelp
②	1 stalk	Green Onion
	4 slices	Ginger
③	3 c.	Skimmed Soup Stock
	½ t.	Salt
	⅛ t.	Pepper
1 stalk		Chopped Garlic Leaves (Illust. ①, ②)
1 T.		Cooking Oil

❶ Clean cabbage and cut into segments (1.5 cm) scald in boiling water until soft; set aside. Soak black mushrooms in hot water until soft; remove stems and cut into halves.

❷ Heat casserole and add 1 T. oil. Stir-fry ② until fragrant; add ③ and bring to a boil. Place all of ① on top of cabbage and again bring to boil; simmer over low heat for approximately 20 minutes. Garnish with garlic leaves prior to serving.

■ Calculation of measurements used in table are based on the E.P. method.

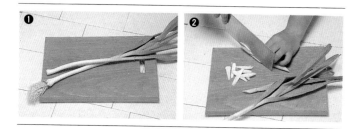

材料 Material	項目 Item 份量，重量 （公克） Unit./Wt. (g)	熱　量 （卡） Energy (Cal.)	蛋白質 （公克） Prot. (g)	脂　肪 （公克） Fat (g)	醣　類 （公克） CHO (g)
大白菜 Nappa Cabbage	600	84	7.8	1.2	15
豆腐 Tender Bean Curd	1塊 PC. 100	65	6.4	4.2	1.8
胡蘿蔔 Carrot	30	11.1	0.3	0.12	2.4
筍 Bamboo Shoots	60	11.4	1.56	0.3	1.44
海帶捲 Rolled Kelp	180	41.4	1.8	0.36	9.54
油 Cooking Oil	1大匙 T. 15	135	0	15	0
合　計 Total		347.9	17.9	21.2	30.2
一人份 Per Serving		58.0	3.0	3.5	5.0

材料：
絲瓜(圖1)‧‧‧‧‧‧‧‧‧‧‧ 1條
(約500公克)
老豆腐‧‧‧‧‧‧‧‧‧‧‧‧ 1½塊
干貝(圖2)‧‧‧‧‧‧‧‧‧‧‧1個
葱(切段)‧‧‧‧‧‧‧‧‧‧‧‧ 1枝
油‧‧‧‧‧‧‧‧‧‧‧‧‧‧‧‧ 1大匙
水‧‧‧‧‧‧‧‧‧‧‧‧‧‧‧‧ 1大匙

① 塩‧‧‧‧‧‧‧‧‧‧‧ 1小匙
麻油‧‧‧‧‧‧‧‧‧‧ ¼小匙
胡椒粉、味精‧‧‧‧‧‧‧
‧‧‧‧‧‧‧‧‧‧各⅛小匙

❶ 將絲瓜去頭尾及外皮(淨重約300公克)，切成長條狀(約0.5×2.5公分)，浸在冷水中，備用。老豆腐切成細絲狀(約0.5×2公分)備用。

❷ 小碗中入干貝及水1大匙，用電鍋蒸至軟(約20分鐘)，趁熱撕成細絲備用。

❸ 鍋熱入油1大匙，爆香葱、干貝，續加已瀝乾的絲瓜以小火煮至七分熟(約3分鐘)；然後將絲瓜劃至鍋的一邊，加入豆腐煮至入味(約3分鐘)，再加入①料，拌勻即成。

■ 為求美觀入味，可將絲瓜炒至熟(約5分鐘)，撈出後餘汁留鍋中，續入豆腐及①料以小火煮至入味(約5分鐘)，再加絲瓜拌勻也可。

■ 重量採可食部份之重量。

INGREDIENTS:

500g (1 lb 1½ oz)	Summer Squash (Illust. ①)
1½ square (5⅓ oz)	Bean Curd
1 pc.	Dried Scallop (Illust. ②)
1 stalk	Green Onion
1 T.	Cooking Oil
1 T.	Water

①
1 t.	Salt
¼ t.	Sesame Oil
⅛ t.	Pepper

❶ Pare and remove tip and end of squash. Cut into long, thin strips (approx. 0.5×2.5cm). Keep immersed in cold water until ready to use. Cut bean curd into thin strips (approx. 0.5×2cm) and set aside.

❷ Wash scallop and place in a small bowl. Add 1 T. water and steam until soft (about 20 minutes). While still warm, finger-shred and set aside.

❸ Heat wok and add 1 T. oil. Stir-fry green onion and shredded scallop until fragrant. Drain squash and stir into wok. Mix and simmer over low heat for about 3 minutes. Gently shift squash to side of wok (away from heat). Add bean curd and simmer until flavor absorbed (about 3 minutes). Season with ①. Gently mix squash with bean curd and serve.

■ Alternative to step ❸ (for better appearance and flavor): Heat wok and add 1 T. oil. Stir-fry green onion and shredded scallop until fragrant. Add drained squash and stir-fry until done (about 5 minutes). Remove and set aside. Place bean curd into wok and stir over low heat. Season with ① and simmer until flavor absorbed (about 5 minutes). Add pre-cooked squash, gently mix and serve.

■ Calculation of measurements used in table are based on the E.P. method.

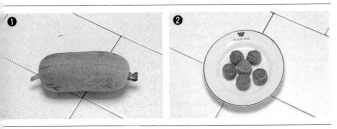

項目 Item / 材料 Material	份量，重量 (公克) Unit/Wt. (g)	熱量 (卡) Energy (Cal.)	蛋白質 (公克) Prot. (g)	脂肪 (公克) Fat (g)	醣類 (公克) CHO (g)
絲瓜 Summer Squash	300	42	3.3	0.6	8.4
老豆腐 Bean Curd	1½ 塊 PC. 150	97.5	9.6	6.3	2.7
干貝 Dried Scallop	1 個 PC. 10	31.4	6.17	0.2	0.78
油 Cooking Oil	1 大匙 T. 15	135	0	15	0
麻油 Sesame Oil	¼ 小匙 t. 1.25	11.25	0	1.25	0
合計 Total		317	19.1	23.4	11.9
一人份 Per Serving		53	3.2	3.9	2.0

涼拌干絲 Beancurd Noodle and Celery Salad

材料：
干絲（圖1）………150公克
芹菜………………30公克
胡蘿蔔……………30公克
① { 水………………4杯
    小蘇打………1小匙

② { 塩…………… ¾小匙
    麻油………… ½小匙
    味精、胡椒粉 ⅛小匙

❶芹菜洗淨切段，胡蘿蔔切絲，全部入沸水中川燙約3
  秒。
❷干絲切段（圖2），①料煮沸入干絲馬上熄火泡5分鐘
  至干絲變軟即可撈出泡冷水除去小蘇打味，再瀝乾使
  用。
❸最後將干絲、芹菜、胡蘿蔔絲及②料拌勻即成。
■重量採可食部份之重量。

INGREDIENTS:

150g (5¼ oz)	Bean Curd Noodles (Illust. ①)	
30g (1 oz)	Celery	
30g (1 oz)	Carrot	
① { 4 c.	Water	
{ 1 t.	Baking Soda	
② { ¾ t.	Salt	} Dressing
{ ½ t.	Sesame Oil	
{ ⅛ t.	Pepper	

❶ Wash and trim celery; cut into 2-inch strips. Shred
  carrot. Scald celery and carrot strips in boiling
  water for 30 seconds. Remove and drain.
❷ Make a few cuts in bean curd noodles to shorten
  (Illust. ②). Bring ① to a boil and add bean curd
  noodles. Immediately turn off heat and let stand
  for 5 minutes. When bean curd softens, remove
  and plunge into cold water. Rinse several times
  to remove baking soda odor. Drain and set aside.
❸ Mix bean curd noodles, celery and carrot strips
  together with ②. Toss and serve.
■ Calculation of measurements used in table are
  based on the E.P. method.

材料 Material	項目 Item	份量，重量 （公克） Unit/Wt. (g)	熱 量 （卡） Energy (Cal.)	蛋白質 （公克） Prot. (g)	脂 肪 （公克） Fat (g)	醣 類 （公克） CHO (g)
干絲 Bean Curd Noodles		150	150	14.55	9.9	4.05
芹菜 Celery		30	0.3	0.24	0.03	0.6
胡蘿蔔 Carrot		30	1.1	0.3	0.12	2.4
油 Cooking Oil		½小匙 2.5 t.	22.5	0	2.5	0
合 計 Total			173.9	15.1	12.6	7.1
一人份 Per Serving			29	2.5	2.1	1.2

材料：

素腸(圖1)‥‥‥‥300公克
香菇‥‥‥‥‥‥‥‥‥ 2朵
① { 油‥‥‥‥‥‥ 1大匙
    麻油‥‥‥‥‥¼小匙

薑‥‥‥‥‥‥‥‥‥‥10片
水‥‥‥‥‥‥‥‥‥‥ 1杯
② { 純釀醬油‥ 1½大匙
    代糖、胡椒粉‥‥‥‥
    ‥‥‥‥‥‥各¼小匙
    味精‥‥‥‥‥⅛小匙

❶素腸洗淨，切斜片(圖2)，香菇以水泡軟，去蒂，切斜片備用。
❷鍋熱入①料，爆香薑片、香菇，隨入素腸拌炒數下，再入水及②料，以小火燜煮 5～10 分至汁略收乾即成。
■素腸為植物性蛋白質來源。

INGREDIENTS:

300g (10½ oz)	Vegetarian Rolls (Su-Tsang) (Illust. ①)
2	Dried Black Mushrooms
10 slices	Ginger
1 c.	Water
① { 1 T.	Cooking Oil
¼ t.	Sesame Oil
② { 1½ T.	Soysauce
¼ t.	Sugar Substitute
¼ t.	Pepper

❶ Wash vegetarian rolls and slice diagonally (Illust. ②). Soak mushrooms in warm water, trim off stems and slice at a slant.

❷ Heat wok and add ①. Stir-fry ginger and mushroom slices until fragrant. Stir in vegetarian rolls. Add 1 cup water and blend in ②. Cook over low heat for 5-10 minutes, or until sauce is reduced to half.

■ Su-Tsang is derived from vegetable protein.

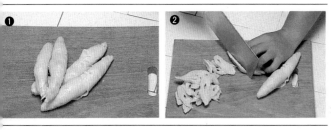

項目 Item 材料 Material	份量‧重量 (公克) Unit/Wt. (g)	熱 量 (卡) Energy (Cal.)	蛋白質 (公克) Prot. (g)	脂 肪 (公克) Fat (g)	醣 類 (公克) CHO (g)
素腸 Vegetarian Rolls	300	342	53.7	0.6	33.6
香菇 Dried Black Mushrooms	2 朵 PC. 10	12.9	1.3	0.17	5.9
油 Cooking Oil	1 大匙 T. 15	135	0	15	0
麻油 Sesame Oil	¼ 小匙 t. 1.25	11.25	0	1.25	0
合 計 Total		501	55	17	39.5
一人份 Per Serving		84	9.2	2.8	6.6

素菜捲 Vegetable Rolls

材料：

高麗菜…6大片(180公克)
白蘿蔔…………220公克
胡蘿蔔…………75公克
木耳……………30公克
紅辣椒……………1條
薑絲……………1大匙

① 白醋………1½大匙
麻油………1大匙
味精、胡椒粉
………各⅛小匙
鹽…………¾小匙

❶高麗菜入滾水中川燙至軟，撈出瀝乾備用。
❷白蘿蔔、胡蘿蔔、木耳、紅辣椒切絲，白蘿蔔加½小匙鹽，胡蘿蔔加¼小匙鹽，各醃約10分鐘後，去水，備用。
❸除高麗菜外，所有材料均加①料拌勻，醃約半小時後分成六等分，每一等分以燙好之高麗菜捲成春捲狀(圖1)，每一菜捲再切成兩半即成。(圖2)
■重量採可食部份之重量。

INGREDIENTS:

6 large sheets (180g/6⅓ oz) Cabbage Leaves
220g (8 oz)   Pared Turnip
75g (2⅔ oz)   Carrot
30g (1 oz)   Dried Fungus (Black Wood Ear)
1   Red Pepper
1 T   Shredded Ginger
¾ t.   Salt

① { 1½ T.   White Vinegar
    1 T.   Sesame Oil
    ⅛ t.   Pepper

❶ Parboil cabbage leaves until softened. Remove and drain.
❷ Shred turnip, carrot, wood-ear and red pepper into thin strips. Separately marinate shredded turnip with ½ t. salt, and shredded carrot with ¼ t. salt, for approximately 10 minutes. Drain and dry by patting with paper towel. Set aside.
❸ Mix all pre-shredded vegetables with ① and marinate for ½ hour. Divide into 6 portions. Place 1 portion filling onto each cabbage leaf and wrap into shape of spring rolls (Illust. ①). Cut each roll in half and serve on platter (Illust. ②).
■ Black wood-ear should be pre-soaked in warm water for 15 minutes. Discard stems (hard ends).
■ Calculation of measurements used in table are based on the E.P. method.

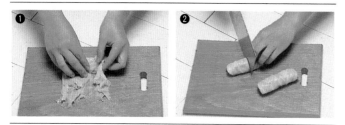

項目 Item 材料 Material	份量，重量 (公克) Unit/Wt. (g)		熱量 (卡) Energy (Cal.)	蛋白質 (公克) Prot. (g)	脂肪 (公克) Fat (g)	醣類 (公克) CHO (g)
高麗菜 Cabbage	180		30.6	3.42	0.18	5.58
白蘿蔔 White Turnip	220		59.4	2.86	0.22	13.2
胡蘿蔔 Carrot	75		27.75	0.75	0.3	6.0
木耳 Dried Fungus	30		33.9	3.03	0.36	19.02
油 Cooking Oil	1 大匙 T.	15	135	0	15.0	0
合計 Total			287	10	16.1	43.8
一人份 Per Serving			48	1.7	2.7	7.3

蒜泥菠菜 Spinach With Garlic Sauce

材料：

菠菜(淨重)	……………………	300公克
水	……………………	6杯

① {
冷開水	……………………	4大匙
純釀醬油	……………………	1大匙
蒜泥	……………………	2小匙
麻油	……………………	½小匙
味精	……………………	⅛小匙

❶菠菜去蒂(淨重300公克)洗淨，切段備用。
❷水6杯燒滾，入菠菜煮至熟，撈出瀝乾水份置盤，淋上
　①料即成。
■菠菜含維他命A 31500國際單位(5250國際單位/人)
　菠菜含維他命C 180毫克(30毫克/人)
■重量採可食部份之重量。

INGREDIENTS:

300g (10½ oz)	Spinach	
6 c.	Water	

① {
4 T.	Water	
1 T.	Soysauce	Seasoning Sauce
2 t.	Mashed Garlic	
½ t.	Sesame Oil	

❶ Trim spinach; cut off root ends. Wash and cut into segments.
❷ Boil 6 cups water and parboil spinach. Remove, drain and place on serving plate. Pour seasoning sauce ① on top and serve.
■ Calculation of measurements used in table are based on the E.P. method.
■ Spinach contains Vitamin A 31500 I.U. (5250 I.U./person) Vitamin C 180mg (30mg/person).

項目 Item 材料 Material	份量・重量 (公克) Unit/Wt. (g)	熱　量 (卡) Energy (Cal.)	蛋白質 (公克) Prot. (g)	脂　肪 (公克) Fat (g)	醣　類 (公克) CHO (g)
菠菜 Spinach	300	48	6.9	0.6	7.2
油 Cooking Oil	½ 小匙 t. 2.5	22.5	0	2.5	0
合　計 Total		70.5	6.9	3.1	7.2
一人份 Per Serving		11.8	1.2	0.5	1.2

材料：

青江菜‥‥‥‥‥‥ 300公克
香菇(大)‥‥‥‥‥‥ 7朵
油‥‥‥‥‥‥‥‥ 1大匙

① 麻油、酒‥各½小匙
  塩‥‥‥‥‥‥ ⅜小匙
  味精‥‥‥‥‥ ¼小匙

② 水‥‥‥‥‥‥ 1½杯
  醬油‥‥‥‥‥ 2大匙
  麻油、酒‥各½小匙
  味精‥‥‥‥‥ ⅛小匙

❶ 青江菜對切洗淨，入滾水川燙至熟(約1分鐘)撈出，趁熱加①料拌勻，排於圓盤圍邊。

❷ 將香菇泡軟去蒂，對切斜刀，備用。

❸ 鍋熱入油1大匙，爆香香菇再入②料以小火煮至入味(約5分鐘)，然後起鍋，擺於盤中心即成。

■ 青江菜含維他命A16200國際單位(2700國際單位/人)
  青江菜含維他命C156毫克(26毫克/人)

■ 重量採可食部份之重量。

INGREDIENTS:

300g (10½ oz)	Chinese Green Cabbage (bok choy)
7	Large Dried Black Mushrooms
1 T.	Cooking Oil

① { ½ t. Sesame Oil / ½ t. Cooking Wine / ⅜ t. Salt

② { 1½ c. Water / 2 T. Soysauce / ½ t. Sesame Oil / ½ t. Cooking wine

❶ Wash green cabbage (bok choy) and halve each stalk lengthwise. Blanch in boiling water until cooked (approx. 1 minute); drain. While still warm, add ① and mix well. Arrange around rim of serving plate.

❷ Soak mushrooms in hot water, discard stems and cut into halves at an angle; set aside.

❸ Heat wok; add 1 T. oil and stir-fry mushrooms until fragrant. Add ②, stir and simmer over low heat for approximately 5 minutes. Remove and place at center of serving plate.

■ Calculation of measurements used in table are based on the E.P. method.

■ Chinese Green Cobbage (Bok Choy) contains Vitamin A 16200 I.U. (2700 I.U./person) Vitamin C 156mg (26mg/person)

材料 Material	項目 Item / 份量，重量 (公克) Unit/Wt. (g)	熱量 (卡) Energy (Cal.)	蛋白質 (公克) Prot. (g)	脂肪 (公克) Fat (g)	醣類 (公克) CHO (g)
青江菜 Chinese Green Cabbage	300	42	6.0	0.3	6.6
香菇 Dried Black Mushrooms	7 朵 PC. 40	51.6	5.2	0.68	23.6
油 Cooking Oil	1 大匙 T. 15	180.0	0	20.0	0
酒 Wine	1 小匙 t. 5	5	0	0	—
麻油 Sesame Oil	1 小匙 t. 5	45	0	5	0
合計 Total		323.6	11.2	26.0	30.2
一人份 Per Serving		54	1.9	4.3	5.0

紅燒筍　Saucy Bamboo Shoots

材料：

綠竹筍(圖1)‥‥‥600公克
菠菜‥‥‥‥‥‥‥ 150公克
柴魚(圖2)‥‥‥‥‥2大匙

① { 水‥‥‥‥‥‥‥‥ 3杯
　　純釀醬油‥‥‥ 3大匙
　　味精‥‥‥‥‥⅛小匙

② { 水‥‥‥‥‥‥‥ 1小匙
　　麻油、太白粉‥‥‥‥
　　　　‥‥‥‥各½小匙
　　代糖‥‥‥‥‥⅛小匙

❶將筍去殼洗淨，切塊(淨重約300公克)，菠菜去蒂頭，洗淨切段入滾水川燙至熟(約30秒鐘)，撈出瀝乾，排在盤的四周備用。

❷鍋熱，入①料燒滾後，加柴魚及筍塊，以小火煮至熟(約15分鐘)，然後取出筍，排在盤中，湯汁過濾，去柴魚渣，加②料勾芡淋在菜上即成。

■菠菜含維他命A 15750國際單位(2625國際單位/人)
■重量採可食部份之重量。

INGREDIENTS:

600g (1 lb 5 oz)		Bamboo Shoots (Illust. ①)
150g (5¼ oz)		Spinach
2 T.		Shredded Dried Stock Fish (Illust. ②)
①	3 c.	Water
	3 T.	Soysauce
②	1 t.	Water
	½ t. each:	Sesame Oil, Cornstarch
	⅛ t.	Sugar Substitute

❶ Remove skin from bamboo shoots, wash and cut into bite-size pieces (net weight approx. 300g). Cut off roots from spinach, wash and cut into segments; parboil for about 30 seconds; drain and arrange around rim of serving plate.

❷ Heat wok, add ① and bring to a boil. Add dried stock fish, bamboo shoots and cook over low heat until done (about 15 minutes). Remove shoots (leaving liquid in wok) and place in center of serving plate. Strain liquid (discard stock fish); re-heat and stir in ② to thicken. Pour sauce on bamboo shoots and serve.

■ Calculation of measurements used in table are based on E.P. method.

■ Spinach contains: Vitamin A 15750 I.U. (2625 I.U./person).

材料 Material \ 項目 Item	份量,重量 (公克) Unit/Wt. (g)		熱量 (卡) Energy (Cal.)	蛋白質 (公克) Prot. (g)	脂肪 (公克) Fat (g)	醣類 (公克) CHO (g)
綠竹筍 Bamboo Shoots	300		57	7.8	1.5	7.2
菠菜 Spinach	150		24	3.45	0.3	3.6
油 Cooking Oil	½ 小匙 t.	2.5	22.5	0	2.5	0
合計 Total			104	11.25	4.3	10.8
一人份 Per Serving			17	1.9	0.7	1.8

材料：

絲瓜	900公克	油 …… 1大匙
里肌肉	40公克	水 …… ½杯
① 水 …… ½小匙		② 塩 …… ½小匙
醬油 …… 1小匙		味精 …… ⅛小匙

❶絲瓜去皮，去籽，去果肉，切3×1.5公分片狀備用
（處理後淨重350公克）
❷里肌肉切薄片，以①料醃10分鐘。
❸鍋熱入油1大匙，再入絲瓜拌炒數下，隨入半杯水，煮
開加蓋改小火燜煮半小時，即入醃好的里肌肉及②料
拌炒至肉熟即成。
■重量採可食部份之重量。

INGREDIENTS:

900g (2 lb)		Summer Squash
40g (1⅓ oz)		Pork Loin
1 T.		Cooking Oil
½ c.		Water
①	½ t.	Water
	1 t.	Soysauce
②	½ t.	Salt

❶ Pare and core squash. Slice into 3×1.5cm pieces (net weight approx. 350g).
❷ Cut pork into thin slices and marinate with ① for 10 minutes.
❸ Heat wok and add 1 T. oil. Briskly stir-fry sliced squash, and add ½ c. water. Bring to a boil, cover and simmer for ½ hour. Add marinated pork slices and mix in ②. Keep stirring until pork is thoroughly cooked. Serve.
■ Summer Squash may be replaced by Zucchini.
■ Calculation of measurements used in table are based on E.P. method.

材料 Material ＼ 項目 Item	份量，重量（公克）Unit/Wt. (g)	熱量（卡）Energy (Cal.)	蛋白質（公克）Prot. (g)	脂肪（公克）Fat (g)	醣類（公克）CHO (g)
絲瓜 Summer Squash	350	49	3.85	0.7	9.8
里肌肉 Pork Loin	40	138.8	5.84	12.64	—
油 Cooking Oil	1 大匙 T 15	105.96	0	11.99	0
合計 Total		293.8	9.7	25.3	9.8
一人份 Per Serving		49.0	1.6	4.2	1.6

材料：
綠蘆筍‥‥‥‥‥‥‥‥‥‥‥‥‥‥‥ 600公克
水‥‥‥‥‥‥‥‥‥‥‥‥‥‥‥‥‥‥‥‥ 6杯
① { 塩、麻油、酒‥‥‥‥‥各½小匙
{ 味精‥‥‥‥‥‥‥‥‥‥‥‥‥⅛小匙

❶綠蘆筍去老皮（淨重500公克），洗淨切段。
❷6杯水燒開，入蘆筍燙熟，撈起瀝乾，再與①料拌勻
即成。
■重量採可食部份之重量。

INGREDIENTS:

600g (1 lb 5 oz)　Fresh Green Asparagus
6 c.　　　　　　　Water
① { ½ t. each:　　Salt, Sesame Oil
{ 　　　　　　　 Cooking Wine

❶ Wash and trim asparagus; cut into segments.
❷ Parboil asparagus with 6 c. of water. Remove and drain. Mix in ①. Toss and serve.
■ Calculation of measurements used in table are based on E.P. method.

材料 Material	份量・重量 (公克) Unit/Wt. (g)	熱 量 (卡) Energy (Cal.)	蛋白質 (公克) Prot. (g)	脂 肪 (公克) Fat (g)	醣 類 (公克) CHO (g)
綠蘆筍 Green Asparagus	500	100	10	1	20
油 Cooking Oil	½ 小匙 t. 2.5	22.5	0	2.5	0
合 計 Total		122.5	10	3.5	20
一人份 Per Serving		20	1.7	0.6	3.3

材料：

鷄蛋	3個	
皮蛋(圖1)	2個	
熟鹹蛋(圖2)	1個	

① { 水 ⋯⋯⋯⋯⋯ ½杯
　　塩 ⋯⋯⋯⋯⋯ ³⁄₈小匙
　　味精 ⋯⋯⋯⋯ ¼小匙

❶皮蛋、熟鹹蛋去殼，切小丁(0.5公分四方)備用。

❷鷄蛋加①料，用筷子攪勻，再將切好之鹹蛋、皮蛋放入拌勻，即倒在方型便當盒中，再用蒸鍋以小火蒸10分鐘，至蛋熟，食時倒出切塊即成。

■選擇皮蛋的方法：買皮蛋時，注意蛋的外殼有無黑點，無黑點的皮蛋均未加鉛、銅製成，有黑點的皮蛋多利用鉛塩、銅塩製造。

■蛋爲最優良的蛋白質來源。

■重量採可食部份之重量。

INGREDIENTS:

3	Eggs
2	Limed Eggs (1000 Year-Old Eggs) (Illust. ①)
1	Cooked Salted Eggs (Illust. ②)
① { ½ c.	Water
⅜ t.	Salt

❶ Peel salted and limed eggs. Dice into 0.5 cm cubes.

❷ Beat fresh eggs and stir in ①. Mix with diced eggs and pour into mold (approx. 10×15cm). Steam over medium heat until firm (about 10 minutes). Cool and invert mold to remove. Slice and serve.

■ Egg is the best source of protein.

■ Calculation of measurements used in table are based on E.P. method.

材料 Material \ 項目 Item	份量·重量 （公克） Unit/Wt. (g)	熱 量 （卡） Energy (Cal.)	蛋白質 （公克） Prot. (g)	脂 肪 （公克） Fat (g)	醣 類 （公克） CHO (g)
鷄蛋 Eggs	3 個 PC. 150	259.5	18.75	19.2	1.2
皮蛋 Limed Eggs	2 個 PC. 100	179	14.5	12.0	2.0
熟鹹蛋 Cooked Salted Eggs	1 個 PC. 50	113	7.05	8.45	1.6
合 計 Total		551.5	40.3	39.7	4.8
一人份 Per Serving		92.0	6.7	6.6	0.8

材料：

鶏蛋⋯⋯⋯⋯⋯⋯⋯ 4個	
番茄(紅)⋯⋯⋯ 160公克	
葱花⋯⋯⋯⋯⋯⋯ 2大匙	
油⋯⋯⋯⋯⋯⋯⋯ 1大匙	

① 塩⋯⋯⋯⋯⋯³⁄₄小匙
麻油⋯⋯⋯⋯¹⁄₂小匙
味精、胡椒粉⋯⋯⋯
⋯⋯⋯⋯⋯各⅛小匙

❶番茄去蒂洗淨，切末，鶏蛋打散備用。
❷鍋熱入油1大匙，爆香葱花，入番茄丁及①料炒勻，再入蛋汁，以小火烘成蛋餅(約4分鐘)即成。
■重量採可食部份之重量。

INGREDIENTS:

4		Eggs
160g (5½ oz)		Ripe Tomatoes
2 T.		Chopped Green Onion
1 T.		Cooking Oil
①	¾ t.	Salt
	½ t.	Sesame Oil
	⅛ t.	Pepper

❶ Wash tomatoes, remove stems and mince. Beat eggs and set aside.

❷ Heat wok and add 1 T. oil. Add chopped green onions, tomatoes and ① (in that order); stir-fry and mix well. Pour in eggs and simmer over low heat until omelet is formed (approx. 4 minutes).

■ Calculation of measurements used in table are based on E.P. method.

材料 Material	項目 Item 份量，重量 (公克) Unit/Wt. (g)	熱 量 (卡) Energy (Cal.)	蛋白質 (公克) Prot. (g)	脂 肪 (公克) Fat (g)	醣 類 (公克) CHO (g)
鶏蛋 Eggs	4 個 PC. 200	346	25	25.6	1.6
番茄 Ripe Tomatoes	160	28.8	1.12	0.48	5.6
油 Cooking Oil	1 大匙 T. 15	135	0	15	0
麻油 Sesame Oil	1 小匙 t. 2.5	22.5	0	2.5	0
合 計 Total		532	26.1	43.6	72
一人份 Per Serving		89	4.4	7.3	1.2

材料：

老豆腐……3塊（300公克）
魚肉………………75公克
絞肉………………37公克
豆苗………………37公克
葱末、薑末……各1小匙

① 水……………1大
太白粉………1小
酒……………½小
塩、醬油…各¼小
味精…………⅛小

② 酒、塩……各1小
麻油…………½小
味精、胡椒粉……各⅛小

高湯(去油)…………6

❶豆腐洗淨，每塊切成6小塊，每小塊中央以湯匙挖個小洞，上灑太白粉備用，豆苗也洗淨備用。

❷將魚肉洗淨剁碎，拌入絞肉、葱末、薑末及①料，分成18等分塞入豆腐中，備用。

❸高湯燒滾，改小火，入已塞肉的豆腐煮至熟(約3分鐘)，續入豆苗及②料即成。

■重量採可食部份之重量。

INGREDIENTS:

3 squares (10½ oz) Bean Curd
75g (2⅔ oz) Fish Fillet
37g (1⅓ oz) Ground Pork
37g (1⅓ oz) Spinach
1 t. Minced Green Onion
1 t. Minced Ginger

①
1 T. Water
1 t. Cornstarch
½ t. Cooking Wine
¼ t. Salt
¼ t. Soysauce

②
1 t. each: Cooking Wine, Salt
½ t. Sesame Oil
⅛ t. Pepper
6 c. Skimmed Soup Stock

❶ Rinse bean curd and cut each square into equal portions. Create a cavity in each pie by scooping out the center with a spoon. Sprinkle with cornstarch and set aside. Wash spinach

❷ Clean fish fillet and mince; stir in ground por together with minced green onion and ginger Mix thoroughly with ①. Divide mixture into 1 equal portions and stuff one portion into each of the previously prepared bean curd pieces

❸ Bring soup stock to a boil. Lower heat and gentl place stuffed bean curd pieces into soup. Simme over low heat till done (approx. 3 minutes). Add spinach and whisk in ②.

■ Calculation of measurements used in table are based on E.P. method.

項目 Item / 材料 Material	份量・重量（公克）Unit/Wt. (g)		熱量（卡）Energy (Cal.)	蛋白質（公克）Prot. (g)	脂肪（公克）Fat (g)	醣類（公克）CHO (g)
豆腐 Bean Curd	3 塊 PC.	300	195	19.2	12.6	5.4
魚肉 Fish Fillet		75	96.75	12.15	4.8	0.45
絞肉 Ground Pork		37	203.13	4.55	20.28	—
豆苗 Spinach		37	—	—	—	—
太白粉 Cornstarch	1 小匙 t.	5	16.86	0.06	0.02	4
油 Cooking Oil	½ 小匙 t.	2.5	22.5	0	2.5	0
合計 Total			534.2	36.0	40.2	9.9
一人份 Per Serving			89.0	6.0	6.7	1.7

枸杞虱目魚湯　Fish Soup With Chinese Herbs

材料：
虱目魚……1尾（600公克）
枸杞（圖1）2大匙（35公克）
當歸（圖2）……………1片
薑………………………3片
水………………………5杯

① { 塩…………… 1小匙
    酒…………… ½小匙

❶將虱目魚處理乾淨（淨重約12兩），切成6塊放入大碗中
　備用。
❷加枸杞、當歸、薑片、水於大碗中，然後將蒸鍋內水
　燒開，以大火蒸至魚肉熟後（約15分鐘），取出加①料
　，即可食用。
■處理虱目魚時，魚肚內的油必須去除乾淨，以免食入
　過多的油脂。

INGREDIENTS:

600g (1 lb 5 oz)	Milk Fish
35g (1¼ oz)	Wolfberry Leaves (Illust. ①)
1 slice	Chirata (Dang Guei) (Illust. ②)
3 slices	Ginger
5	Water
① { 1 t.	Salt
½ t.	Cooking Wine

❶ Wash and clean milk fish thoroughly (net weight approx. 12 oz); cut into 6 pieces and place in large soup bowl. Add wolfberry leaves, chirata, ginger slices and 5 cups water into bowl. Place bowl into steamer and steam over high heat until done (about 15 minutes). Remove from steamer, stir in ① and serve.

■ While cleaning fish, it is advisable to trim off fat from belly in order to minimize fat consumption.

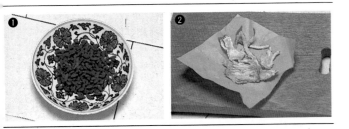

項目 Item 材料 Material	份量・重量 （公克） Unit/Wt. (g)	熱 量 （卡） Energy (Cal.)	蛋白質 （公克） Prot. (g)	脂 肪 （公克） Fat (g)	醣 類 （公克） CHO (g)
虱目魚 Milk Fish	1 尾 PC. 600	468	80.4	10.8	7.2
枸杞 Wolfberry Leaves	35	9.45	1.5	0.28	0.91
合 計 Total		477	81.9	11.1	8.1
一人份 Per Serving		80	13.7	1.8	1.4

羅宋湯 Russian Borscht

材料：

牛腩	300公克	
高麗菜	300公克	
洋蔥	60公克	
胡蘿蔔	60公克	
紅番茄	150公克	
油	1大匙	

① 葱‧‧‧‧2枝(切段)
　 薑‧‧‧‧2片
　 水‧‧‧‧16杯
② 塩‧‧‧‧1小匙
　 味精‧‧‧‧⅛小匙

❶牛腩洗淨切塊，用乾鍋炒至變色(可去血水)。

❷高麗菜、洋蔥、胡蘿蔔及番茄全部洗淨切塊，番茄用
1大匙油炒軟備用。

❸將牛腩、洋蔥加①料煮沸後改小火煮至八分熟，再入
胡蘿蔔、高麗菜，共煮至牛腩軟爛熄火，待涼後，冰
凍除去上面的油。

❹去油的全料再次煮開後加入炒好的番茄及②料即成。
■如嫌酸者，可把番茄籽擠掉。
■高麗菜含維他命C 120毫克(20毫克/人)
■重量採可食部份之重量。

INGREDIENTS:

300g (10½ oz)		Beef
300g (10½ oz)		Cabbage
60g (2 oz)		Onions
60g (2 oz)		Carrots
150g (5¼ oz)		Tomatoes
1 T.		Cooking Oil
①	2 stalks	Green Onion (cut into segments)
	2 slices	Ginger
	16 c.	Water
②	1 t.	Salt

材料 Material	項目 Item	份量，重量 （公克） Unit/Wt. (g)	熱量 （卡） Energy (Cal.)	蛋白質 （公克） Prot. (g)	脂肪 （公克） Fat (g)	醣類 （公克） CHO (g)
牛腩 Beef		300	399	56.4	17.4	—
高麗菜 Cabbage		300	51	5.7	0.3	9.3
洋蔥 Onion		60	15	0.54	0.24	3.0
胡蘿蔔 Carrot		60	22.2	0.6	0.24	4.8
紅番茄 Tomatoes		150	27	10.5	0.45	5.25
油 Cooking Oil		1 大匙 T. 15	135	0	15	0
合 計 Total			749	73.7	33.6	22.4
一人份 Per Serving			125	12.3	5.6	3.7

❶ Wash beef and cut into chunks (2.5cm³). Parch
in dry wok over medium heat until pale. Remove
and set aside.

❷ Wash cabbage, onions, carrots and tomatoes;
cut into cubes. Heat wok, add 1 T. oil and stir-fry
tomatoes until soft. Set aside for later use.

❸ Bring ① to a boil; add beef and onions, lower
heat and simmer for about 1 hour. Add carrots
and cabbage; continue to simmer until beef is
tender (about 1½ hour). Turn off heat, cool and
refrigerate. Skim off fat.

❹ Re-heat skimmed soup and bring to a boil. Add
pre-cooked tomatoes and mix in ②.

■ If a less sour taste is preferred, remove seeds
from tomatoes before stir-frying.

■ Calculation of measurements used in table are
based on E.P. method.

■ Cabbage contains Vitamin C 120mg (20mg/
person)

材料：
草魚中段‧‧‧‧‧‧‧‧‧‧‧‧‧‧‧‧‧‧‧‧ 300公克
菠菜(淨重)‧‧‧‧‧‧‧‧‧‧‧‧‧‧‧‧‧‧ 150公克
薑‧‧‧‧‧‧‧‧‧‧‧‧‧‧‧‧‧‧‧‧‧‧‧‧‧‧‧‧‧‧ 5片
葱‧‧‧‧‧‧‧‧‧‧‧‧‧‧‧‧‧‧‧‧‧‧‧‧‧‧‧‧‧‧ 1枝
① ┌ 水‧‧‧‧‧‧‧‧‧‧‧‧‧‧‧‧‧‧‧‧‧‧‧‧ 6杯
　 │ 塩‧‧‧‧‧‧‧‧‧‧‧‧‧‧‧‧‧‧‧‧‧‧ 1小匙
　 │ 味精‧‧‧‧‧‧‧‧‧‧‧‧‧‧‧‧‧‧ ¼小匙
　 └ 胡椒粉‧‧‧‧‧‧‧‧‧‧‧‧‧‧ ⅛小匙

❶草魚洗淨，去皮去骨切薄片(圖1)(淨重225公克)，薑片切絲、葱切絲。
❷菠菜去根洗淨(淨重150公克)切段，放在大湯碗內，再排上魚片。
❸將①料煮開放入薑、葱絲後沖入湯碗內即成(圖2)。

INGREDIENTS:

300g (10½ oz)		Fish Fillet
150g (5¼ oz)		Spinach
5 slices		Shredded Ginger
1 stalk		Shredded Green Onion
①	6 c.	Water
	1 t.	Salt
	⅛ t.	Pepper

❶ Clean fish and cut into very thin slices (Illust. ①).
❷ Trim spinach, wash and cut into segments. Place into large soup bowl. Lay fish slices on top of spinach (slices should not overlap each other). Bring ① to a boil and add shredded green onion and ginger. Pour over fish into soup bowl. Serve immediately (Illust. ②).

項目 Item 材料 Material	份量，重量 (公克) Unit/Wt. (g)	熱　量 (卡) Energy (Cal.)	蛋白質 (公克) Prot. (g)	脂　肪 (公克) Fat (g)	醣　類 (公克) CHO (g)
草魚 Fish Fillet	225	299	52.9	7.7	1.35
菠菜 Spinach	150	24	3.45	0.3	3.6
合　計 Total		323	56.4	8	5
一人份 Per Serving		54	9.4	1.3	0.8

腎臟病的飲食治療

　　腎臟好比是清道夫，它主要作用是將肝臟分解蛋白質所產生的含氮廢物排出體外，以維持血液的正常組成和容量，當腎功能開始發生病變時，腎臟對廢物的處理效率也漸漸減低；當廢物不能被有規律的排出體外時，就堆積在血液中，使腎臟的負荷大為加重，如此會繼續進展成為慢性腎衰竭及尿毒症。

　　腎功能不全是漸進式的，若能在早期發現並給予適當治療，可減慢其進展至尿毒症之速度，飲食治療在此即佔重要角色，正確的飲食控制可減少體內廢物的產生以減輕腎臟的負荷，欲減少廢物的堆聚，必須限制蛋白質的量及攝取足夠的熱量，而攝取量之多少必須依病情而定，所以在此僅提出此類飲食之重要注意原則，詳細飲食設計必須請營養師為您個別設計，飲食原則：

1. 植物性高蛋白食物因其生理價值低應禁忌
   a. 豆腐、豆干、豆漿等豆製品。
   b. 麵筋、麵腸、烤麩等麵筋製品。
   c. 黃豆、毛豆、綠豆、紅豆、蠶豆、豌豆仁等豆類。
   d. 瓜子、核桃、腰果、杏仁、花生等核果類。

2. 高磷食物應禁忌
   如：酵母、全穀類、內臟、蛋黃、牛奶、豆類及堅果類等。

3. 每日准許攝取的蛋白質量中，至少須有75％來自高生理價值的蛋白質，如蛋白及肉類食物。

4. 米麵類及其製品，蔬菜、水果均含有相當量的低生理價值的植物性蛋白，不可隨意食用，請依照營養師為您設計的量食用。

5. 每日所需熱量，可由下列含熱量高且蛋白質極低的食物補足，如：益富糖飴、白糖、冰糖、蜂蜜、薑糖、水果糖、植物性油脂(如大豆油)及低氮澱粉類(如：益富米粒、益富米粉、澄粉、玉米粉、太白粉、藕粉、冬粉、涼粉、粉皮、西谷米、粉圓)，以彌補因在限制蛋白質原則下，所造成的熱量攝取不足。

6. 若有高血壓及水腫需配合限鈉飲食，則應禁食任何醃製、罐頭及各種加工食品，調味品限用塩及醬油，可攝取量須依營養師指示食用，或採用益富醬油。

7. 每日須補充維生素及礦物質(由醫師指示服用)。

8. 肉類如先用水撈煮後再用油炒、煎、炸可除去更多的磷，可使每日磷的攝入量減至500毫克以下，大約為一般不限制飲食的$\frac{1}{3}$至$\frac{1}{4}$。

9. 依病情需要而須同時採用低鈉、低鉀飲食，甚至還須限制水分的食入量，這些限制均須由醫師決定，絕對不要自行作主。

Dietary Therapy for Chronic Renal Failure

The kidney is similar to a garbage disposal. Its main function is to excrete nitrogen-containing waste matters formed when protein is metabolized in the body, in order to maintain a normal composition and volume of blood. When renal function begins to impair, its efficiency in excreting waste matters is hindered. When waste matters cannot be excreted regularly, they accumulate in the blood, causing the kidney to become over-burdened. If unattended, chronic renal failure and uremia may develop as a result.

If impairment of renal function is discovered during its early stage, and suitable therapy is prescribed, the rate of its development into uremia can be retarded. Diet therapy plays an important role herein. A correct dietary regimen can reduce the production of waste matters in the body, thus, lessening the workload of the kidney. In order to reduce the accumulation of waste matter, the amount of protein must be restricted and adequate energy must be consumed. The quantity of protein allowed is determined by the severity of the illness. As a result, only some important principles are introduced below. A detailed dietary regimen must be individually designed by a dietitian. Some dietary principles to observe:

1. Low-biological value protein foods should be avoided.
   a. Soybean products, such as beancurds, dried beancurds, soybean milk.
   b. Gluten products, such as gluten, gluten rolls, grilled gluten.
   c. Beans, such as soybeans, beans, mung beans, red beans, broad beans, peas.
   d. Seeds and nuts, such as watermelon seeds, walnuts, cashew nuts, almonds, peanuts.
2. Foods with high phosphorus content should be avoided, such as yeasts, whole-grain cereal, organ meats, eggyolk, milk, beans and nuts.
3. Among daily consumption of protein permitted, at least 75% should come from foods with high-biological value, such as eggwhite and meats.
4. Rice, noodles and their bi-products, vegetables, fruits containing large amounts of vegetable protein of low-biological value, should not be consumed at will; quantity should be designated by a dietitian.
5. Adequate energy may be supplemented with the following: foods with high-energy content but low-protein content, such as E. F. Nutri-Powder (hydrolyzed starch), sugar, candy, honey, ginger sugar, vegetable oil (e.g., soybean oil) and low-nitrogen starch, such as E.F. rice (protein-free rice) E.F. rice noodles (protein-free rice noodles), tapioca, cornstarch, whole-wheat starch, lotus root starch, bean thread, agar-agar, bean thread sheets and sago, in order to compensate for the inadequacy of energy consumption caused by protein restrictions.
6. If sodium is also restricted because of high blood pressure and/or edema, preserved, canned and all processed foods should be avoided. Flavorings, salt and soysauce should be limited to a quantity prescribed by a dietitian. E.F. soysauce (low-sodium, low-potassium) may be used.
7. Vitamin and mineral supplements should be taken daily as prescribed by a physician.
8. If meat is boiled before stir-frying, frying or deep-frying, excess phosphate can be eliminated. Daily phosphorus consumption may be reduced to below 500mg which is 1/3 to 1/4 of that obtained from a regular diet.
9. In severe cases, low-sodium and low-potassium foods should be used. Restriction of water consumption is also sometimes necessary. All these restrictions should be stipulated by your physician. NEVER MAKE JUDGMENTS ON YOUR OWN.

Frances C. Ma

材料：

內餡
蝦仁…………75公克
荸薺…………100公克
香菇末·¼杯（20公克）
香菜末…………¼杯
油…………1½大匙

外皮
澄粉…………½杯
太白粉………5大匙
滾開水………¾杯

① {
酒、太白粉各½大匙
糖、麻油…各1小匙
塩、胡椒粉各¼小匙
}

❶ 將蝦仁去腸泥洗淨切小丁，荸薺也洗淨切小丁備用。

❷ 鍋熱入油1½大匙，炒香香菇末，續入蝦仁、荸薺、香菜末及①料炒至熟，即成"內餡"。

❸ 將外皮的所有材料攪拌均勻後，揉成麵糰，分成24等份（每份10公克），每個外皮包8公克的內餡，再以手揑成"餃子"狀即可。

❹ 將作成的水晶餃，入滾水（約6杯），煮至熟（約5分鐘即可食用。

■ 如果蛋白質限制較嚴格時，可以一兩的五花肉，代替蝦仁；如此亦可達到熱量的需求。

INGREDIENTS:

Filling:

75g (2⅔ oz)	Raw Shelled Shrimp
100g (3½ oz)	Chopped Water Chestnuts
¼ c.	Chopped Dried Black Mushroom (pre-soaked)
¼ c.	Chopped Coriander
1½ T.	Cooking Oil

Wrapping:

½ c.	Wheat Starch
5 T.	Cornstarch
¾ c.	Hot Water
① ½ T. each:	Cooking Wine, Cornstarch
1 t. each:	Sugar, Sesame Oil
¼ t. each:	Salt, Pepper

❶ Rinse and devein shrimp; chop and set aside.

❷ Filling: Heat wok, then add 1½ T. oil. Stir-fry chopped mushrooms until fragrant; add chopped shrimp, water chestnuts, coriander and ①. Stir-fry until done.

❸ Wrapping: Blend all ingredients and knead into smooth dough. Divide dough into 24 portions (each portion approx. 10g). Flatten pieces of dough by hand, and using rolling pin, shape into small thin pancakes.

❹ Place a portion of filling (about 8g) in center of each flattened piece of dough and fold over, slightly moisten outer edges with water and pinch together to seal. Repeat until all 24 dumplings are formed.

❺ Bring 6 cups water to boil and gently drop dumplings in. Keep boiling until done (about 5 minutes). Drain and serve.

■ In cases where protein intake must be strictly restricted, shrimp may be substituted with 37g pork side, which contains comparable caloric values.

材料 Material	份量·重量 Unit/Wt. (g)	熱量 Energy (Cal.)	水份 H₂O (g)	蛋白質 Prot. (g)	脂肪 Fat (g)	糖類 CHO (g)	鈉 Na (mg)	鉀 K (mg)	磷 P (mg)
蝦仁 Shrimp	75	65.25	59.85	13.80	0.53	0.30	138.8	249.8	138
荸薺 Water Chestnuts	100	64	80	1.10	0.10	15.6	16		80
香菇 Mushrooms	2朵 PC. 20	25.80	3.04	2.60	0.34	11.80	2.8	82.8	22.8
油 Cooking Oil	1½大匙 T. 22	194.26	0	0	21.98	0			
澄粉 Whole Wheat Flour	½杯 PC. 65	219.05	—	0.81	0.16	52	3.9	5.85	0
太白粉 Cornstarch	5大匙 T. 75	252.75	—	0.94	0.19	60	3.9	5.85	0
水 Water	¾杯 C. 180	0	180	0	0	0			
酒 Wine	½大匙 T. 7	—	7	—	—	—	5	5	
糖 Sugar	1小匙 t. 5	20	—	0	0	5			
麻油 Sesame Oil	1小匙 t. 5	44.15	0	0	5	0	0	—	—
塩 Salt	¼小匙 t. 1	0	0.07	0	0	0	390	0.04	
合計 Total		885	330	19.3	28.3	144.7	560.4	349.3	240.8
一人份 Per Serving		442	165	9.6	14.2	72.4	280.2	174.6	120.4

香菇米粉　Stir-Fried Rice Noodle With Black Mushrooms

材料：

盆富米粉	80公克	油	3大匙
綠豆芽	300公克	水	1/2杯
韭菜	30公克	醬油	2小匙
五花肉絲	50公克	麻油、太白粉	
香菇	2朵	① 各1小匙	
油葱	1大匙	糖、酒 各1/2小匙	
水	6杯	塩	1/4小匙
		胡椒粉	1/8小匙

❶ 將盆富米粉，加6杯水，以小火煮至熟（約40分鐘），撈出備用。

❷ 綠豆芽摘去頭尾（約150公克），洗淨，韭菜洗淨、切段，香菇泡軟去蒂、切絲，備用。

❸ 鍋熱入油3大匙，爆香油葱，續入香菇、五花肉絲，炒至熟，再入已煮熟的盆富米粉、①料、綠豆芽、韭菜，拌炒至熟即成。

■ 盆富米粉主要成份是小麥澱粉、玉米澱粉，100公克盆富米粉，含熱量348卡、蛋白質0.3公克、醣類86.4公克、脂肪0公克、鈉2.6毫克，是專為腎臟病人製作的米粉。

■ 綠豆芽150公克，是採E.P.(指可食用部份)，盆富米粉80公克煮熟後、吸水量為300公克。

INGREDIENTS:

80g	(2¾ oz)	Protein-free Rice Noodles
300g	(10½ oz)	Green Bean Sprouts
30g	(1 oz)	Leeks
50g	(1¾ oz)	Shredded Pork Side or Belly
2		Dried Black Mushrooms
1 T.		Shallots
6 c.		Water
3 T.		Cooking Oil

①	½ c.	Water
	2 t.	Soysauce
	1 t. each:	Sesame Oil, Cornstarch
	½ t. each:	Sugar, Cooking Wine
	¼ t.	Salt
	⅛ t.	Pepper

❶ Bring 6 cups water to a boil; add protein-free rice noodles and cook over low heat until done (about 40 minutes). Drain and set aside.

❷ Wash and trim bean sprouts (net weight about 150g). Wash leeks and cut into segments. Soak mushrooms, trim off stems and shred. Set aside.

❸ Heat wok and add 3 T. oil; stir-fry shallots until fragrant; add shredded mushrooms and pork strips. Stir-fry until cooked. Stir in pre-cooked protein-free rice noodles and add ①, followed by bean sprouts and leeks. Keep mixing in wok until done.

■ Protein-free rice noodles consist mainly of starch derived from wheat and corn, and has been formulated especially for people with kidney disorders. Every 100g of protein-free rice noodles contains 348 calories; protein -- 0.3g; sugar -- 86.4g; Fat -- 0; sodium -- 2.6 mg.

項目 Item / 材料 Material	份量・重量 (公克) Unit/Wt. (g)	熱量 (卡) Energy (Cal.)	水份 (公克) H₂O (g)	蛋白質 (公克) Prot. (g)	脂肪 (公克) Fat (g)	醣類 (公克) CHO (g)	鈉 (毫克) Na (mg)	鉀 (毫克) K (mg)	磷 (毫克) P (mg)
盆富米粉 P. F. Rice Noodles	80	278.4	—	0.24	0	69.12	2.08	5.68	16.2
綠豆芽 G. Bean Sprouts	150	22.5	142.8	2.7	0.15	3	7.5	352.5	97.5
韭菜 Leeks	30	5.1	27.99	0.66	0.12	0.66	1.8	70.2	19.8
五花肉 Pork	50	274.5	16.2	6.15	27.4	—	28	134	131
香菇 Mushrooms	2朵 PC. 10	12.9	1.52	1.3	0.17	5.9	1.4	41.4	11.4
油 Cooking Oil	3大匙 T. 45	450	0	0	50	0	—	—	—
糖 Sugar	½小匙 t. 2.5	9.5	0.03	0	0	2.46	—	—	—
水 Water	300	0	30	0	0	0	0	—	—
醬油 Soysauce	2小匙 t. 10	4.4	7.28	0.62	0.1	0.36	630	38.6	11.4
太白粉 Cornstarch	1小匙 t. 5	16.85	—	0.06	0.02	4	—	0.4	0
酒 Wine	½小匙 t. 2.5	—	2.5	—	—	—	—	1.8	—
塩 Salt	¼小匙 t. 1.25	—	i	—	—	—	487.5	0.1	—
合計 Total		1074	228.3	11.7	78	85.5	1158.3	644.7	287.3
一人份 Per Serving		179	38.1	2	13	14.3	193	107.4	47.9

四寶飯 Four-Treasure Rice

6人份
serves

材料：

盒富米粉30根(約40公克)
米……………………30公克
青椒…………………30公克
洋葱…………………30公克
胡蘿蔔………………20公克
五花肉絲……………30公克

油…………………… 2大
水…………………… 3¼

① 醬油………… 1小
麻油…………½小
糖……………¼小
鹽……………⅛小

❶將盒富米粉加3杯水，放冰箱浸泡一夜，撈出切粒狀
用。
❷將米洗淨入¼杯水和已泡軟的米粉粒拌勻，再入電
中(外鍋加¼杯水)煮至熟即成米飯，備用。
❸將青椒、洋葱、胡蘿蔔切小丁備用。
❹鍋熱入油2大匙，爆香洋葱，續入五花肉絲及胡蘿蔔
至熟，再拌入已煮熟的米飯、①料及青椒丁即可食
。

■胡蘿蔔之維生素A含量達433國際單位(RDA: 6000
際單位)，盒富米粉40公克浸泡後，吸水量約150毫升

項目 Item / 材料 Material	份量·重量 (公克) Unit/Wt. (g)	熱量 (卡) Energy (Cal.)	水份 (公克) H_2O (g)	蛋白質 (公克) Prot. (g)	脂肪 (公克) Fat (g)	醣類 (公克) CHO (g)	鈉 (毫克) Na (mg)	鉀 (毫克) K (mg)	磷 (毫克) P (mg)
盒富米粉 P. F. Rice Noodles	40	139.2	—	0.12	0	34.56	1.04	2.8	8.1
米 Rice	30	106.2	4.02	1.95	0.15	23.43	114.3	8.7	18.6
青椒 Green Pepper	30	4.8	28.08	0.3	0.06	0.99	3.9	61.8	6
洋葱 Onion	30	7.5	27.75	0.27	0.12	1.5	3	45	12
胡蘿蔔 Carrot	20	7.4	17.42	0.2	0.08	1.6	4.4	57.6	4.4
五花肉 Pork	30	164.7	9.72	3.69	16.44	—	16.8	80.4	78.6
油 Cooking Oil	2 大匙 T. 30	2.70	0	0	30	0	—	—	—
糖 Sugar	¼ 小匙 t. 1.25	4.75	0.02	0	0	1.23	—	—	—
鹽 Salt	⅛ 小匙 t. 0.62	0	0.04	0	0	0	241	—	—
醬油 Soysauce	1 小匙 t. 5	2.2	3.64	0.31	0.05	0.18	315	19.3	5.7
水 Water	210	—	210	—	—	—	—	—	—
麻油 Sesame Oil	½ 小匙 t. 2.5	22.5	0	0	2.5	—	—	—	—
合計 Total		729	300.7	6.8	49.4	63.4	592	275.6	133.4
一人份 Per Serving		121.5	50.1	1.13	8.23	10.5	98.6	45.9	22.2

INGREDIENTS:

40g (1⅓ oz)	Protein-free Rice Noodles
30g (1 oz)	Rice
30g (1 oz)	Green Bell Pepper
30g (1 oz)	Onion
20g (⅔ oz)	Carrot
30g (1 oz)	Shredded Pork Side or Belly
2 T.	Cooking Oil
3¼ c.	Water
① 1 t.	Soysauce
½ t.	Sesame Oil
¼ t.	Sugar
⅛ t.	Salt

❶ Soak Protein-free rice noodles in 3 cups wate until soft. Refrigerate overnight. Drain and chop

❷ Rinse rice until water runs clear; drain. Add ¼ cup water and mix in pre-soaked chopped ric noodles; stir until well-mixed. Pour ¼ cup wate into outer layer of rice cooker. Cook rice an noodle mixture until done.

❸ Wash and dice green pepper, onion and carro Set aside.

❹ Heat wok and add 2 T. oil; stir-fry onion unt fragrant; add pork and diced carrots, stirrin until cooked. Mix in pre-cooked rice and noodl mixture; season with ① and add diced gree pepper. Stir quickly and serve.

材料：

粉絲‥‥‥‥ 1把(50公克)
香菇‥‥‥‥‥‥‥‥ 2朵
小黃瓜‥‥‥‥‥‥50公克
胡蘿蔔‥‥‥‥‥‥30公克
薑絲‥‥‥‥‥‥‥ 2大匙
油‥‥‥‥‥‥‥‥ 4大匙

①
水‥‥‥‥‥‥ 1½杯
醬油‥‥‥‥‥ 1大匙
酒、麻油‥‥各½小匙
塩、糖、黑醋、胡椒
粉‥‥‥‥‥‥各¼小匙

❶將冬粉泡軟、瀝乾，香菇洗淨泡軟去蒂、切絲，小黃瓜去頭尾切絲，胡蘿蔔切絲均備用。

❷鍋熱入油4大匙，爆香薑絲，續入香菇、胡蘿蔔、粉絲，炒勻後入①料，以小火煮至粉絲熟爛(約3分鐘)，再拌入小黃瓜，即可起鍋。

■胡蘿蔔之維生素A含量達650國際單位(RDA：6000國際單位)

INGREDIENTS:

50g (1¾ oz)	Bean Threads (1 bunch)
2	Dried Black Mushrooms
50g (1¾ oz)	Gherkin Cucumber
30g (1 oz)	Carrot
2 T.	Shredded Ginger
4 T.	Cooking Oil

①
1½ c.	Water
1 T.	Soysauce
½ t. each:	Cooking Wine, Sesame Oil
¼ t. each:	Salt, Sugar, Dark Vinegar, Pepper

❶ Soak bean threads in water until soft, then drain. Wash and soak mushrooms, cut off stems and shred. Trim off tip and end of cucumber; wash and shred. Trim carrot and shred. Set aside.

❷ Heat wok and add 4 T. oil; stir-fry shredded ginger until fragrant. Add mushrooms, carrots and bean threads. Mix well. Season with ① and continue stir-frying over low heat until bean threads soften (about 3 minutes). Add shredded cucumber, mix and serve.

項目 Item / 材料 Material	份量・重量 Unit/Wt. (g)	熱量 (卡) Energy (Cal.)	水份 (公克) H₂O (g)	蛋白質 (公克) Prot. (g)	脂肪 (公克) Fat (g)	醣類 (公克) CHO (g)	鈉 (毫克) Na (mg)	鉀 (毫克) K (mg)	磷 (毫克) P (mg)
冬粉 Bean Threads	1把 PC. 50	173	7.2	0.10	0.05	42.35	—	69.5	10
香菇 Mushrooms	2朵 PC. 20	25.8	3.04	2.60	0.34	11.8	2.8	82.8	22.8
小黃瓜 Cucumber	50	5	48.2	0.45	0.05	1.00	2.5	78	9
胡蘿蔔 Carrot	30	11.1	26.3	0.30	0.12	2.40	6.6	86.4	6.6
水 Water	1½杯 C. 360	0	360	0	0	0	0	0	0
薑絲 Ginger	2大匙 T. 20	7.4	17.6	0.26	0.08	1.54	1.4	63.2	6.4
油 Cooking Oil	4大匙 T. 60	540	0	0	60	0	—	—	—
醬油 Soysance	1大匙 T. 15	6.6	10.92	0.93	0.15	0.54	945	57.8	17.1
塩 Salt	¼小匙 t. 1.25	—	0.07	0	0	0	390	0.04	—
糖 Sugar	¼小匙 t. 1.25	4	—	0	0	1	—	—	—
黑醋 D. Vinegar	¼小匙 t. 1cc	—	—	—	—	—	—	1	0.3
麻油 Sesame Oil	½小匙 t. 2.5	22.5	—	0	2.5	0	—	—	—
合計 Total		795.4	473.2	5.6	63.3	60.6	1348.3	438.7	72.2
一人份 Per Serving		132.6	78.9	0.9	10.6	10.1	224.7	72.9	12

材料：
青江菜⋯⋯⋯⋯ 150公克
草菇⋯⋯⋯⋯⋯ 150公克
五花肉⋯⋯⋯⋯ 50公克
太白粉⋯⋯⋯⋯ ½杯
地瓜粉⋯⋯⋯⋯ ¼杯
油⋯⋯⋯⋯⋯ 2大匙
葱⋯⋯⋯⋯⋯ 1根

水⋯⋯⋯⋯⋯ ½杯
① { 水⋯⋯⋯⋯⋯ ¾杯
醬油⋯⋯⋯⋯ 1大匙
黑醋、麻油、糖、酒 各1小匙
② { 水⋯⋯⋯⋯⋯ 1小匙
太白粉⋯⋯⋯ ½小匙

❶地瓜粉、太白粉、水混勻，置已抹油之方形鐵盤中，以大火蒸至熟（約25分鐘），取出切片（約1×3公分）即成素海參，備用。
❷青江菜洗淨去葉，剩餘菜梗的部份，對切成長段，草菇切半，五花肉切細絲，葱切段，均備用。
❸青江菜、草菇入滾水中川燙，撈出瀝乾備用。
❹鍋熱入油2大匙，爆香葱段，續入五花肉炒至半熟，再入①料及素海參，以小火煮至入味（約15分鐘），續入草菇、青江菜，煮至熟，最後以②料勾芡即成。
■青江菜之維生素A含量達1350國際單位（RDA：6000國際單位）

INGREDIENTS:

150g (5¼ oz)	Chinese Green Cabbage (Bok Choy)
150g (5¼ oz)	Straw Mushrooms
50g (1¾ oz)	Pork Side or Belly
½ c.	Cornstarch
¼ c.	Sweet Potato Flour
2 T.	Cooking Oil
1 stalk	Green Onion (cut into segments)
½ c.	Water
① { ¾ c.	Water
1 T.	Soysauce
1 t. each:	Dark Vinegar, Sesame Oil, Sugar, Cooking Wine
② { 1 t.	Water } mix
½ t.	Cornstarch }

❶ Mix ¼ cup sweet potato flour and ½ cup cornstarch with ½ cup water. Blend well and pour into lightly greased metal container and steam over high heat until firm (about 25 minutes). Remove and cut into slices (approx. 1×3 cm). This is the vegetarian sea-cucumber.
❷ Wash and trim green cabbage. Cut off leafy ends and halve stalks lengthwise. Wash straw mushrooms and split lengthwise. Shred pork.
❸ Parboil green cabbage and straw mushrooms. Drain and set aside.
❹ Heat wok and add 2 T. oil; stir-fry green onion until fragrant, add shredded pork and continue to stir-fry until half-cooked. Stir in ①, add sea-cucumber slices, and cook over low heat until flavor absorbed (about 15 minutes). Add green cabbage, straw mushrooms and mix. Stir in mixture ② to thicken sauce, and serve.

項目 Item / 材料 Material	份量・重量 (公克) Unit/Wt. (g)		熱量 (卡) Energy (Cal.)	水份 (公克) H₂O (g)	蛋白質 (公克) Prot. (g)	脂肪 (公克) Fat (g)	醣類 (公克) CHO (g)	鈉 (毫克) Na (mg)	鉀 (毫克) K (mg)	磷 (毫克) P (mg)
地瓜粉 Sweet Potato Flour	¼ 杯 C.	37.5	126.38	6.04	0.45	0.11	30	22.5	445	35.6
太白粉 Cornstarch	½ 杯 C.	65	219.1	10.5	0.78	0.2	52	3.9	5.85	0
青江菜 Green Cabbage		150	21	141	3	0.15	3.3	33	—	51
草菇 Mushrooms		150	42	136.95	4.5	0.45	4.8	21	621	171
五花肉 Pork		50	274.5	16.2	6.15	27.4		28	134	131
水 Water	1¼ 杯 C.	300	0	300	0	0	0	—	—	—
醬油 Soysauce	1 大匙 T.	15	6.6	10.92	0.93	0.15	0.54	945	57.8	17.1
黑醋 Dark Vinegar	1 小匙 t.	5	—	5					5	1.3
麻油 Sesame Oil	1 小匙 t.	5	45	0	0	5	0	—	—	—
油 Cooking Oil	2 大匙 T.	30	270	0	0	30	0	—	—	—
糖 Sugar	1 小匙 t.	5	20	—	—	—	5	0.1	5.3	—
酒 Wine	1 小匙 t.	5	—	5	—	—	—	—	3.6	—
太白粉 Cornstarch	1½ 小匙 t.	2.5	8.4	0.4	0.03	0	2	0.15	0.2	0
合計 Total			1033	632.01	15.8	63.5	97.6	1053.7	1273.8	407
一人份 Per Serving			172	105.3	2.6	10.6	16.3	175.6	212.3	67.8

肉絲澄麵湯 Shredded Pork Noodle Soup

6人份
serves 6

材料：

肉絲‥‥‥‥‥‥‥‥60公克
小白菜(切段)‥‥‥100公克
香菇(切絲)‥‥‥‥‥‥2朵
葱(切段)‥‥‥‥‥‥‥2根
油‥‥‥‥‥‥‥‥‥‥2大匙
白油‥‥‥‥‥‥‥‥‥1大匙

① { 澄粉、滾開水 各1杯
     太白粉‥‥‥‥‥‥½杯

② { 高湯‥‥‥‥‥‥‥‥4杯
     塩、麻油‥‥各½小匙
     糖、胡椒粉各¼小匙

❶將①料拌勻後，加入白油、揉成麵糰，以擀麵棍擀成
　薄片，再切成麵條。
❷鍋內入水約6杯，大火煮開再放入麵條煮至熟，撈出備
　用，小白菜川燙備用。
❸鍋熱入油2大匙，炒香葱、香菇，續入②料燒滾，再入
　肉絲、小白菜、澄麵條煮1分鐘即可食用。
■依個人喜好，可以雞絲或魚肉代替肉絲(五花肉絲)。

INGREDIENTS:

60g (2 oz)		Shredded Pork
100g (3½ oz)		Chinese Cabbage (cut into segments)
2		Shredded Dried Black Mushrooms (pre-soaked)
2 stalks		Green Onion (cut into segments)
2 T.		Cooking Oil
1 T.		Vegetable Shortening
①	1 c. each:	Wheat Starch, Hot Water
	½ c.	Cornstarch
②	4 c.	Soup Stock
	½ t. each:	Salt, Sesame Oil
	¼ t. each:	Sugar, Pepper

❶ Blend all ingredients in ①. Add vegetable shortening and knead into a smooth dough. Flatten with rolling pin and cut into long, thin noodle strips.

❷ Bring 6 cups water to a boil, add noodles and cook until done. Drain and set aside. Parboil cabbage, drain and set aside.

❸ Heat wok and add 2 T. oil; stir-fry green onions and mushrooms until fragrant; add ② and bring to a boil. Add shredded pork and cabbage. Stir; add pre-cooked noodles; mix well; cook for 1 minute and serve.

■ Fish or poultry may be substituted for pork.

項目 Item 材料 Material	份量・重量 (公克) Unit/Wt. (g)	熱量 (卡) Energy (Cal.)	水份 (公克) H₂O (g)	蛋白質 (公克) Prot. (g)	脂肪 (公克) Fat (g)	醣類 (公克) CHO (g)	鈉 (毫克) Na (mg)	鉀 (毫克) K (mg)	磷 (毫克) P (mg)
肉絲(五花肉) Pork	60	208.2	31.68	8.76	52.67	—	33.6	160.8	157.2
小白菜 C. Cabbage	100	10	94.8	1.50	0.10	1.50	—	599	58
香菇 Mushrooms	2朵 PC. 20	25.8	3.04	2.60	0.34	11.8	2.8	82.8	22.8
葱 G. Onions	2根 PC. 20	5.4	18.10	0.36	0.06	1.12	3	38.4	8.2
油 Cooking Oil	2大匙 T. 30	265	0	0	30	0	—	—	—
澄粉 Whole Wheat Flour	1杯 C. 130	438.1	—	1.63	0.33	104	7.8	11.7	0
太白粉 Cornstarch	½杯 C. 65	219.05	—	0.81	0.16	52	3.9	5.85	0
白油 Shortening	1大匙 T. 15	132.45	0	0	14.99	0	—	—	—
水 Water	4杯 C. 960	0	0	0	0	0	—	—	—
塩 Salt	½小匙 t. 2.5	—	0.18	—	—	—	975	0.1	—
糖 Sugar	¼小匙 t. 1	4	—	0	0	4	—	—	—
麻油 Sesame Oil	½小匙 t. 2.5	22.5	—	0	2.5	0	—	—	—
合計 Total		1334	1347.8	15.7	101.6	171.4	1074.1	898.7	246.2
一人份 Per Serving		222	224.6	2.6	16.9	28.6	179.0	149.8	41

101

香菇盒子 Mushroom-Capped Taro Balls

材料：

香菇(小)‥‥‥‥‥‥12朵
絞肉(五花肉)‥‥‥‥50公克
芋頭(去皮)‥‥‥‥ 180公克
白油‥‥‥‥‥‥‥‥35公克
油‥‥‥‥‥‥‥‥‥ 2大匙
太白粉‥‥‥‥‥‥ 1½大匙
薑‥‥‥‥‥‥‥‥‥ 2片

炸油‥‥‥‥‥‥‥‥ 5杯
① { 水‥‥‥‥‥‥‥‥¼杯
　 醬油、糖‥‥ 各1小匙
② { 澄粉‥‥‥‥ 1½大匙
　 糖‥‥‥‥‥ ½小匙
　 塩‥‥‥‥‥ ¼小匙

❶香菇洗淨泡軟去蒂，鍋熱入油1大匙，爆香薑片後，入香菇及①料，以小火煮至入味(約5分鐘)，取出香菇上灑太白粉備用。
❷鍋熱入油1大匙，將絞肉炒至熟，備用。
❸芋頭蒸熟(約需20分鐘)趁熱攪成泥，續入白油、②料及已炒熟的絞肉，一起拌勻後，平分成12等分，並捏成圓形備用。
❹將香菇蓋在芋頭上，入已燒熱的炸油中，炸至金黃(約1分鐘)，即成。
■香菇含鉀高，故限鉀者，不宜使用。
■油90公克，是由於烹調中所用的2大匙油，加上香菇盒子炸時所吸的油的總合。
■澄粉1大匙10公克。

INGREDIENTS:

12 (20g/⅔ oz)	Dried Black Mushrooms
50g (1¾ oz)	Ground Pork Side or Belly
180g (6⅓ oz)	Pared Taro
35g (1¼ oz)	Vegetable Shortening
2 T.	Cooking Oil
1½ T.	Cornstarch
2 slices	Ginger
5 c.	Cooking Oil (for deep-frying)
① { ¼ c.	Water
1 t. each:	Sugar, Soysauce
② { 1½ T.	Wheat Starch
½ t.	Sugar
¼ t.	Salt

❶ Soak mushrooms and trim off stems. Heat wok and then add 1 T. oil; stir-fry ginger slices until fragrant; and add mushrooms. Stir in ① and simmer over low heat until flavor is absorbed (about 5 minutes). Remove mushrooms, dredge with 1½ T. cornstarch and set aside.

❷ Heat wok and add 1 T. oil; stir-fry ground pork until done. Set aside.

❸ Steam pared taro over high heat (about 20 minutes) until done. Remove, and while still warm mash into paste. Add pre-fried ground pork, vegetable shortening and ②. Mix thoroughly and divide into 12 portions. Shape into balls and set aside.

❹ Cap each taro ball with a mushroom. Heat 5 cups oil and deep-fry until golden brown. Drain and serve.

■ As Black Mushrooms contain potassium, they are not recommended for use in diets which severely restrict potassium ingestion.

項目 Item／材料 Material	份量・重量 (公克) Unit/Wt. (g)		熱 量 (卡) Energy (Cal.)	水 份 (公克) H₂O (g)	蛋白質 (公克) Prot. (g)	脂 肪 (公克) Fat (g)	糖 類 (公克) CHO (g)	鈉 (毫克) Na (mg)	鉀 (毫克) K (mg)	磷 (毫克) P (mg)
香菇 Mushrooms	12 朵 PC	20	26.41	3.04	2.0	0.34	11.0	2.8	82.9	22.8
絞肉(五花肉) Pork	50		274.5	16.2	4.15	27.4	—	28	134	131
芋頭 Pared Taro	180		201.6	121.14	5.58	0.36	45.36	9	927	108
白油 Shortening	35		315	0	0	35	0	0		
油 Cooking Oil	90		810	0	0	90	0	0		
太白粉 Cornstarch	1½ 大匙 T.	22	74.14	0	0.28	0.06	17.6	1.32	1.98	0
糖 Sugar	1½ 小匙 t.	8	32	—	—	—	8		0.2	0
澄粉 Whole Wheat Flour	1½ 大匙 T.	15	50.55	0	0.19	0.04	12	0.9	1.4	0
醬油 Soysauce	1 小匙 t.	5	2.2	3.64	0.31	0.05	0.18	315	19.3	5.7
塩 Salt	¼ 小匙 t.	1.25	0	0	0	0	0	487.5	—	—
水 Water	¼ 杯 C.	60	0	60	0	0	0	0	0	0
合 計 Total			1786	204.0	12.5	153.3	94.1	844.5	1173.2	267.5
一人份 Per Serving			298	34	2.1	25.5	15.7	140.8	195.5	44.6

蘋 果 捲 Apple Rolls

材料：

五花肉‥‥‥‥‥‥90公克
蘋果(去皮)‥‥‥‥60公克
太白粉‥‥‥‥‥‥¼杯
葱花‥‥‥‥‥‥ 2大匙
炸油‥‥‥‥‥‥ 5杯

① 水‥‥‥‥‥ 1大匙
太白粉‥‥‥ 2小匙
酒、麻油‥ 各1小匙
胡椒粉、塩各⅛小匙

② 水‥‥‥‥‥‥½杯
醋、糖、麻油、醬油
‥‥‥‥各1小匙

③ 水‥‥‥‥‥ 1大匙
太白粉‥‥‥ 1小匙

❶將五花肉冷凍後切成12薄片，入①料醃約10分鐘，備用。
❷蘋果切成12長條(約4×1公分)，浸冷水中(圖1)，備用。
❸將每片肉，包一條蘋果，捲好後沾滿太白粉(圖2)，入已燒熱的油鍋中，炸至金黃(約3分鐘)，撈出、瀝乾，置盤中備用。
❹鍋熱入油1大匙，爆香葱，續入②料燒至滾，再以③料勾芡，淋於蘋果捲上，即成。

INGREDIENTS:

90g (3 oz)	Pork Side or Belly
60g	Pared Apple
¼ c.	Cornstarch
2 T.	Chopped Green Onion
5 c.	Cooking Oil (for deep-frying)

①
- 1 T. Water
- 2 t. Cornstarch
- 1 t. each: Cooking Wine, Sesame Oil
- ⅛ t. each: Pepper, Salt

②
- ½ c. Water
- 1 t. each: Vinegar, Sugar, Sesame Oil, Soysauce

③
- 1 T. Water
- 1 t. Cornstarch
} mix

❶ Cut pork into 12 thin slices (should be slightly frozen for easier slicing). Add ① and marinate for 10 minutes. Set aside.

❷ Cut apple into 12 long strips (about 4×1cm). Keep immersed in cold water (to prevent discoloration) until ready to use (Illust. ①).

❸ Drain apple, wrap 1 strip of apple in each pork slice and roll. Coat with cornstarch (Illust. ②). Heat 5 cups oil in wok and deep-fry rolls until golden brown (about 3 minutes). Drain and place on serving plate.

❹ Heat wok then add 1 T. oil; stir-fry chopped green onion until fragrant; add ② to season and bring to a boil. Stir in ③ to thicken sauce. Pour mixture on rolls and serve.

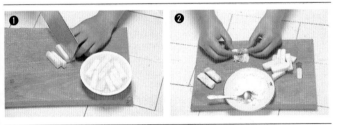

項目 Item／材料 Material	份量，重量 Unit／Wt. (公克)(g)	熱量 Energy (卡)(Cal.)	水份 H₂O (公克)(g)	蛋白質 Prot. (公克)(g)	脂肪 Fat (公克)(g)	醣類 CHO (公克)(g)	鈉 Na (毫克)(mg)	鉀 K (毫克)(mg)	磷 P (毫克)(mg)
五花肉 Pork	90	494.1	29.16	11.07	49.32	—	50.4	241.2	236.3
蘋果 Apple	1 個 PC. 60	23.4	53.1	0.18	0.18	5.88	—	60	6
太白粉 Cornstarch	5 大匙 T. 75	252.74	—	0.94	0.19	60	4.5	6.72	—
油 Cooking Oil	4 大匙 T. 60	540	0	0	60	0	—	—	—
塩 Salt	⅛ 小匙 t. 0.63	—	—	—	—	—	245.7	0.03	—
醬油 Soysauce	1 小匙 t. 5	—	—	—	—	—	315	19.3	5.7
水 Water	120	—	120	—	—	—	—	—	—
合計 Total		1310.5	202.3	12.19	109.74	65.9	615.6	327.25	248
一人份 Per Serving		218.43	33.7	2.03	18.29	10.98	102.6	54.54	41.3

材料：

粉絲	約25公克
香菇(大)	3朵
荸薺、筍	各50公克
胡蘿蔔	30公克
葱末	1大匙
薑末	1小匙
美國生菜	300公克

炸油	6杯
① { 醬油	2小匙
麻油、酒	各1小匙
糖	½小匙
塩	¼小匙
胡椒粉	⅛小匙

❶將冬粉入熱油中，炸至鬆乾(約30秒)，取出趁熱壓碎，置盤中，備用。

❷將荸薺、筍、胡蘿蔔切末；香菇洗淨泡軟去蒂，切末，備用。

❸鍋熱入油3大匙，爆香葱薑，續入香菇、胡蘿蔔、荸薺、筍炒至熟，再加①料拌勻，起鍋淋在冬粉上即成。

❹另美國生菜洗淨後，以手剝成片狀，入滾水中川燙一下(約5秒鐘)，置小盤上，夾鴿鬆食用。

■美國生菜川燙的目的，是使菜中大部分的"鉀"離子能溶於水中，以避免攝取過多的鉀離子，對腎臟病人的病情有影響，故家人共食這道菜時，只要將病人食用的部分燙水即可。

INGREDIENTS:

25g (⅞ oz)	Bean Threads
3	Large Dried Black Mushrooms
50g (1¾ oz)	Water Chestnuts
50g (1¾ oz)	Bamboo Shoots
30g (1 oz)	Carrots
1 T.	Minced Green Onion
1 t.	Minced Ginger
300g (10½ oz)	Lettuce
6 c.	Cooking Oil (for deep-frying)
① { 2 t.	Soysauce
1 t. each:	Sesame Oil, Cooking Wine
½ t.	Sugar
¼ t.	Salt
⅛ t.	Pepper

❶ Heat 6 cups oil in wok and deep-fry bean threads until crispy (about 30 seconds). Drain; while hot, crush and place on serving plate.

❷ Mince water chestnuts, bamboo shoots and carrots. Soak black mushrooms, cut off stems, and mince. Set aside.

❸ Heat wok, add 3 T. oil; stir-fry minced green onion and ginger until fragrant. Add minced mushrooms, carrots, water chestnuts and bamboo shoots. Keep stirring until cooked, add ① and mix thoroughly. Place on top of crushed bean threads and serve.

❹ Wash lettuce leaves. Parboil for about 5 seconds, drain and serve on platter. This is for wrapping minced mixture.

■ For patients with kidney disorders, the amount of potassium contained in fresh lettuce may be substantially reduced by parboiling prior to consumption. When dining with others, only the portion of lettuce to be consumed by the patient requires parboiling.

項目 Item / 材料 Material	份量・重量 (公克) Unit/Wt. (g)	熱量 (卡) Energy (Cal.)	水份 (公克) H₂O (g)	蛋白質 (公克) Prot. (g)	脂肪 (公克) Fat (g)	醣類 (公克) CHO (g)	鈉 (毫克) Na (mg)	鉀 (毫克) K (mg)	磷 (毫克) P (mg)
粉絲 Bean Threads	½把 PC. 25	86.5	3.6	0.05	0.03	21.18	7	34.8	5
香菇 Mushrooms	3朵 PC. 30	38.7	4.56	3.90	0.51	17.7	—	124.3	34.3
荸薺 Water Chestnuts	50	32	40	0.55	0.05	7.8	8	—	40
筍 Bamboo Shoots	50	9.5	46	1.30	0.25	1.20	4.5	265	30
胡蘿蔔 Carrot	30	11.1	26.13	0.30	0.12	2.4	1.5	91.9	9.4
油 Cooking Oil	3大匙 T. 45	397.35	0	0	44.96	0	—	—	—
生菜 Lettuce	300	42	278	5.4	0.3	7.5	27	533.3	66.7
醬油 Soysauce	2小匙 t. 10	4.4	7.28	0.62	0.1	0.36	650	38.6	11.4
塩 Salt	¼小匙 t. 1.25	0	0.09	0	0	0	487.5	—	—
麻油 Sesame Oil	1小匙 t. 5	44.15	0	0	5	0	—	—	27.5
糖 Sugar	½小匙 t. 2.5	10	—	0	0	2.5	—	—	—
酒 Wine	1小匙 t. 5	0	—	0	0	0	—	4.8	0.5
粉絲吸油量 Cooking Oil Absorbed	40	360	—	0	40	—	—	—	—
合計 Total		676	405.7	12.1	91.3	60.6	1185.5	1092.7	224.8
一人份 Per Serving		113	67.6	2.0	15.2	10.1	197.6	182.1	37.5

凉拌洋菜　Tossed Agar-Agar

材料：
洋菜……………15公克
小黃瓜…………80公克
胡蘿蔔…………15公克

① 沙拉油……… 3大匙
麻油………… 2小匙
黑醋、糖…各½小匙
塩…………… ¼小匙

❶洋菜洗淨，以熱水泡至軟(約5分鐘)，備用。
❷小黃瓜、胡蘿蔔切細絲，入①料及洋菜拌勻醃20分鐘，即可食用。

INGREDIENTS:

15g (½ oz)	Agar-Agar
80g (2¾ oz)	Gherkin Cucumber
15g (½ oz)	Carrot

① 3 T. Oil
2 t. Sesame Oil
½ t. each: Dark Vinegar, Sugar
¼ t. Salt

❶ Wash agar-agar and soak in hot water until soft (about 5 minutes). Drain and set aside.
❷ Wash and trim cucumber and carrot. Shred and mix with ①; add agar-agar and toss well. Marinate for 20 minutes and serve.

項目 Item 材料 Material	份量·重量 (公克) Unit/Wt. (g)	熱 量 (卡) Energy (Cal.)	水 份 (公克) H₂O (g)	蛋白質 (公克) Prot. (g)	脂 肪 (公克) Fat (g)	醣 類 (公克) CHO (g)	鈉 (毫克) Na (mg)	鉀 (毫克) K (mg)	磷 (毫克) P (mg)
洋菜 Agar-Agar	15	8	—	—	2	2	17.5	16	3
小黃瓜 Cucumber	80	8	77.12	0.72	0.08	1.6	4	125	15
胡蘿蔔 Carrot	15	5.55	13.07	0.15	0.06	1.2	3.3	43.3	3.3
油 Cooking Oil	3 大匙 T. 45	397.4	0	0	45	0	—	—	—
黑醋 Dark Vinegar	½ 小匙 t. 2.5	—	2.5	—	—	—	—	2.5	0.6
糖 Sugar	½ 小匙 t. 2.5	10	—	—	—	2.5	—	—	—
塩 Salt	¼ 小匙 t. 1.25	—	0.09	—	—	—	487.5	—	—
麻油 Sesame Oil	2 小匙 t. 10	90	0	0	10	0	—	—	—
合 計 Total		519	209.8	0.9	57.1	7.3	512.3	86.8	21.9
一人份 Per Serving		86	35	0.2	9.5	1.2	85.4	14.5	3.7

洋葱濃湯 Onion Soup

材料：

洋葱	300公克
高湯	3½杯
油	3大匙
土司麵包	1塊(30公克)
瑪琪琳	½大匙

① ｛ 黑胡椒、糖各¼小匙
義大利香料、塩……
……各⅛小匙

❶ 洋葱切細絲備用。

❷ 鍋熱入油3大匙，以小火炒至洋葱熟爛(約30分鐘)，續入高湯，以小火熬煮1½小時後，再入①料拌勻備用。

❸ 瑪琪琳塗在土司麵包上，烤箱以200℃(392°F)預熱後，將麵包烤至焦黃(約1分鐘)，再置洋葱湯中即成。

■ 如果家裏沒有烤箱，將瑪琪琳塗在麵包上後，也可用烤麵包機將土司麵包烤至焦黃。

■ 高湯3½杯，以小火熱煮後約剩2杯。

INGREDIENTS:

300g (10½ oz)	Onion
3½ c.	Soup Stock
3 T.	Cooking Oil
1 slice (30g/1 oz)	Bread
½ T.	Margarine
① ¼ t. each:	Black Pepper, Sugar
⅛ t. each:	Italian Seasoning, Salt

❶ Peel and shred onion.

❷ Heat wok add 3 T. oil; sauté onion over low heat until soft (about 30 minutes). Add stock and simmer over low heat for 1½ hours. Add ① to season, mix and set aside.

❸ Spread margarine on bread, toast until golden brown. Float toast on soup and serve.

項目 Item 材料 Material	份量・重量 Unit/Wt. (公克)(g)	熱量 Energy (卡)(Cal.)	水份 H₂O (公克)(g)	蛋白質 Prot. (公克)(g)	脂肪 Fat (公克)(g)	糖類 CHO (公克)(g)	鈉 Na (毫克)(mg)	鉀 K (毫克)(mg)	磷 P (毫克)(mg)
洋葱 Onion	300	75	277.5	2.7	1.2	15	30	450	150
油 Cooking Oil	3 大匙 T. 45	405	0	0	45	0	—	—	—
瑪琪琳 Margarine	½ 大匙 T. 7	50	+	+	6	+	7	1.4	1.4
吐司麵包 Bread	1 片 PC. 30	75.9	1.69	0.48	0.03	2.69	416		3.35
水 Water	2 杯 C. 480	0	480	0	0	0	0	—	—
糖 Sugar	¼ 小匙 t. 1.25	5	—	—	—	1.25	—	—	—
塩 Salt	⅛ 小匙 t. 0.625	0	0	0	0	0	243.7	—	+
合計 Total		611	759.2	3.2	52.2	18.9	696.7	451.4	154.8
一人份 Per Serving		102	126.5	0.5	8.7	3.2	116.1	75.2	25.8

材料：

馬鈴薯(去皮)	300公克
紫菜	3張(7公克)
小黃瓜	60公克
柴魚	1大匙
生菜	6片(60公克)
沙拉醬	3大匙

❶ 馬鈴薯切片蒸熟，趁熱攪成泥，待涼再拌入沙拉醬，分成6份，備用。

❷ 小黃瓜切細絲，分成6份，生菜洗淨擦乾，柴魚切碎，紫菜對切成三角形(圖1)，備用。

❸ 每一份紫菜攤平，上放1片生菜、1份馬鈴薯、1份小黃瓜，再捲成甜筒狀(圖2)，上灑½小匙柴魚即可。

■ 紫菜可放入烤箱內烤一下，或置已燒熱的鍋中烘一下，可使紫菜較香脆可口。

■ 為避免腎臟病患攝取過多的鉀離子，故家人共食這道菜時，請將病人食用部份的生菜川燙一下。

INGREDIENTS:

300g (10½ oz)	Pared Potato
3 sheets (120g/4¼ oz)	Dried Pressed Seaweed (Nori)
60g (2 oz)	Gherkin Cucumber
1 T.	Dried Stock Fish
6 sheets (60g/2 oz)	Lettuce Leaves
3 T.	Mayonnaise

❶ Slice potato and steam until soft. Remove and mash while hot. Allow to cool, and blend in mayonnaise. Divide into 6 portions. Set aside.

❷ Shred cucumber and divide into 6 portions. Wash lettuce leaves, parboil, drain and pat dry. Chop stock fish. Halve seaweed sheets diagonally into triangles (Illust. ①). Set aside.

❸ On each triangular sheet of dried seaweed, place a lettuce leaf, 1 portion mashed potato and 1 portion shredded cucumber. Roll into cones (Illust. ②). Sprinkle chopped stock fish on top of each cone and serve.

■ To freshen dried seaweed sheets, toast lightly prior to rolling.

■ For patients with kidney disorders, the amount of potassium contained in fresh lettuce may be substantially reduced by parboiling prior to consumption. When dining with others, only the portion of lettuce to be consumed by the patient requires parboiling.

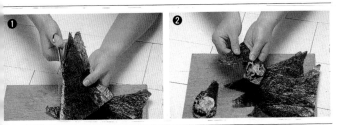

項目 Item / 材料 Material	份量·重量 (公克) Unit/Wt. (g)	熱量 (卡) Energy (Cal.)	水分 (公克) H₂O (g)	蛋白質 (公克) Prot. (g)	脂肪 (公克) Fat (g)	醣類 (公克) CHO (g)	鈉 (毫克) Na (mg)	鉀 (毫克) K (mg)	磷 (毫克) P (mg)
馬鈴薯 Potato	300	225	233.1	6.9	0.3	50.7	6.7	855.6	174
紫菜 Dried Pressed Seaweed	3張 PC. 7	15.82	0.72	1.99	0.06	2.94	—	—	
小黃瓜 Cucumber	60	4.8	58.26	0.3	0.06	0.96	3	93.8	8.4
生菜 Lettuce Leaves	6片 PC. 60	8.4	55.74	1.08	0.06	1.5	6.6	106.7	15
沙拉醬 Mayonnaise	3大匙 T 45	279	10.85	1.8	30.51	0.05	255	14.9	7.2
合計 Total		525	358.7	12.1	31	56.2	271.3	1071	208.7
一人份 Per Serving		88	59.8	2.0	5.2	9.4	45.2	178.5	34.8

三色球 Tri-Colored Balls

材料：

絞肉(五花肉)……90公克
白蘿蔔球‥30顆(240公克)
胡蘿蔔球‥9顆(75公克)
高湯……………1杯
葱(段)……………1根
炸油……………6杯
水……………5杯

① {
太白粉………2小匙
葱末、薑末各½小匙
糖、麻油…各¼小匙
塩、胡椒粉各⅛小匙
}

② {
麻油、酒…各1小匙
塩、糖…各¼小匙
}

③ {
水…………1大匙
太白粉………1小匙
}

❶絞肉加①料拌勻，甩打至有黏性後，用手擠成6個肉丸(圖1)狀，續入已燒熱的炸油中，炸至金黃色(圖2)，撈出瀝乾，備用。

❷水5杯燒至滾，入白蘿蔔、胡蘿蔔，以小火煮至爛(約2小時)，備用。

❸鍋熱入油1大匙，爆香葱後，入肉丸、白蘿蔔、胡蘿蔔、高湯及②料，以小火煮至入味(約3分鐘)，再以③料勾芡即成。

■紅蘿蔔含維生素A 1625國際單位(NRDA：6000 國際單位)

■吸油：指肉丸子油炸之吸油量。

INGREDIENTS:

90g (3 oz)	Ground Pork Side or Belly
240g (8½ oz)	Turnip Balls
75g (2⅔ oz)	Carrot Balls
1 c.	Soup Stock
1 stalk	Green Onion (cut into segments)
6 c.	Cooking Oil (for deep-frying)
5 c.	Water

① {
- 2 t. Cornstarch
- ½ t. each: Minced Ginger, Minced Green Onion
- ¼ t. each: Sugar, Sesame Oil
- ⅛ t. each: Salt, Pepper
}

② {
- 1 t. each: Sesame Oil, Cooking Wine
- ¼ t. each: Salt, Sugar
}

③ {
- 1 T. Water
- 1 t. Cornstarch
} mix

❶ Add ① to ground pork and mix thoroughly. Slap against side of container until slightly sticky. Form 6 balls (Illust. ①). Heat 6 c. oil in wok and deep-fry meat balls until golden brown (Illust. ②). Drain and set aside.

❷ Boil 5 c. water; drop turnip and carrot balls. Cook over low heat until done (about 2 hours). Drain and set aside.

❸ Heat wok add 1 T. oil; stir-fry green onion until fragrant. Add pre-cooked pork, turnip and carrot balls, 1 c. soup stock and ②. Simmer over low heat until flavor absorbed (about 3 minutes). Stir in mixture ③ to thicken sauce and serve.

項目 Item 材料 Material	份量·重量 Unit/Wt. (公克)(g)	熱量 Energy (卡)(Cal.)	水份 H₂O (公克)(g)	蛋白質 Prot. (公克)(g)	脂肪 Fat (公克)(g)	醣類 CHO (公克)(g)	鈉 Na (毫克)(mg)	鉀 K (毫克)(mg)	磷 P (毫克)(mg)
五花肉 Ground Pork	90	494.1	29.16	11.07	49.32	—	50.4	241.2	235.8
白蘿蔔 Turnip	240	36	225.84	1.68	0.24	7.44	52.8	693.4	52.8
紅蘿蔔 Carrot	75	27.75	65.33	0.75	0.3	6	16.5	216	16.5
油 Cooking Oil	1 大匙 T. 15	135	0	0	15	0	—	—	—
太白粉 Cornstarch	1 大匙 T. 15	50.55	—	0.19	0.04	12	0.9	1.35	14.25
塩 Salt	⅛ 小匙 t. 0.625	—	—	—	—	—	733.2	—	+
麻油 Sesame Oil	1¼ 小匙 t. 6.25	56.3	0	0	6.25	0	—	—	—
＊吸油 Cooking Oil Absorbed	1 大匙 T. 15	135	0	0	15	0	—	—	—
糖 Sugar	½ 小匙 t. 2.5	10	—	—	—	2.5	0.03	0.06	0
合計 Total		945	320.3	13.7	86.2	27.9	853.8	1152	319.4
一人份 Per Serving		157.5	53.4	2.3	14.4	4.7	142.3	192	53.2

材料：

牛蒡（淨重）（圖1）180公克
薑…………………… 4片
油………………… 3大匙
水………………… ¼杯

① { 糖…………… 3大匙
    白醋………… 2大匙

② { 水…………… 1小匙
    太白粉……… 1小匙

❶牛蒡切絲泡水（圖2），薑片切絲備用。

❷鍋熱入油3大匙，爆香薑絲，入牛蒡拌炒數下，隨入①料及水¼杯，煮開後改小火燜煮半小時，再以②料勾芡即可。

■使用牛蒡的目的，是由於其富含纖維質。

INGREDIENTS:

180g (6⅓ oz)	Burdock (Illust. ①)
4 slices	Ginger
3 T.	Cooking Oil
¼ c.	Water

① { 3 T. — Sugar
    2 T. — Vinegar

② { 1 t. — Water }
    1 t. — Cornstarch } mix

❶ Pare and shred burdock. To prevent discoloration, keep immersed in cold water (Illust. ②) until ready to use. Shred ginger slices.

❷ Heat wok and 3 T. oil; stir-fry shredded ginger until fragrant; add burdock and stir-fry briskly. Season with ① and add ¼ c. water. Bring to a boil, cover and simmer over low heat for ½ hour. Stir in ② to thicken sauce and serve.

■ Burdock is recommended because of its high fiber content.

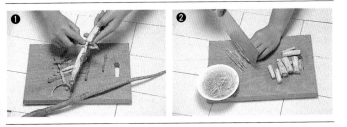

材料 Material	份量・重量 Unit/Wt. (g)	熱量 (卡) Energy (Cal.)	水份 (公克) H₂O (g)	蛋白質 (公克) Prot. (g)	脂肪 (公克) Fat (g)	糖類 (公克) CHO (g)	鈉 (毫克) Na (mg)	鉀 (毫克) K (mg)	磷 (毫克) P (mg)
牛蒡 Burdock	180	133.2	138.6	4.5	0.18	30.96	54	324	104.4
薑 Ginger	4 片 PC. 10	3.7	8.8	0.13	0.04	0.77	0.7	31.6	3.2
油 Cooking Oil	3 大匙 T. 45	405	0	0	45	0	—	—	—
水 Water	¼ 杯 C. 60	0	60	0	0	0	—	—	—
糖 Sugar	3 大匙 T. 45	180	0	—	—	45	0.45	1.1	0
白醋 Vinegar	2 大匙 T. 30	3.3	28.7	0.27	—	0.6	+	30	7.5
太白粉 Cornstarch	1 小匙 t. 5	16.9	—	0.06	0.01	4	0.3	0.45	0
合計 Total		642	236.1	5	45.2	81.3	55.5	387.2	115.1
一人份 Per Serving		107	39.4	0.8	7.5	13.6	9.3	64.5	19.2

材料：

蕃薯(去皮)……	400公克
洋葱圈…………	30公克
香菜葉…………	6片
油………………	6杯

① 太白粉、澄粉各¾杯
　水………………¼杯
　細糖………… 6大匙
　白醋………… 3大匙

❶蕃薯去頭尾及皮，再切6圓片，各片中間切一刀，使成蕃薯夾(圖1)，續將洋葱圈分成6份，分別塞入各個蕃薯夾內(圖2)，備用。

❷①料拌勻成糊狀，鍋熱入油6杯，蕃薯夾沾上①料之麵糊，入油鍋中，炸至熟，撈出，備用。

❸將已炸熟的蕃薯夾，再沾一次麵糊，上面並貼一片香菜葉入熱油中，炸至金黃色，即成。

■限鉀者，不可用蕃薯，可以馬鈴薯代之。

■蕃薯之維生素A含量達 4733 國際單位(RDA：6000國際單位)

■太白粉1杯150公克，1杯澄粉130公克。

■油指炸薯餅之吸油量。

INGREDIENTS:

400g (14 oz)	Sweet Potatoes
30g (1 oz)	Onion Rings
6	Coriander Leaves
6 c.	Cooking Oil (for deep-frying)

① ¾ c. each: Cornstarch, Wheat Starch
　¼ c. Water
　6 T. Confectioner's Sugar
　3 T. Vinegar

❶ Pare and trim potato. Cut horizontally into 6 circular slices. Slit open sides without cutting all the way through. Divide onion rings into 6 portions and stuff into potato slices. Set aside.

❷ Mix ali of ① and stir to make pasty batter. Heat wok and add 6 cups oil; dip stuffed potato pieces in batter and deep-fry until cooked. Remove and drain.

❸ Dip potato pieces again in remaining batter. Garnish each piece with a coriander leaf. Reheat oil and deep-fry again until golden brown. Drain and serve.

■ In diets where potassium intake is severely restricted, sweet potatoes should be replaced with regular potatoes.

項目 材料 Material	份量·重量 (公克) Unit/Wt. (g)	熱 量 (卡) Energy (Cal.)	水 份 (公克) H₂O (g)	蛋白質 (公克) Prot. (g)	脂 肪 (公克) Fat (g)	醣 類 (公克) CHO (g)	鈉 (毫克) Na (mg)	鉀 (毫克) K (mg)	磷 (毫克) P (mg)
蕃薯 Sweet Potatoes	400	452	278	9.2	1.2	103.2	46	1907.6	184.8
洋葱 Onion	30	7.5	27.75	0.27	0.12	1.5	3	45	12
糖 Sugar	6 大匙 T. 90	342	1.26	0	0	90	0.9	2.25	—
太白粉 Cornstarch	¾ 杯 C. 112.5	379.1	—	1.4	0.28	90	6.75	10.1	0
澄粉 Whole Wheat Flour	¾ 杯 C. 97.5	328.6	—	1.2	0.24	78	5.85	8.8	—
白醋 Vinegar	3 大匙 T. 45	279	10.85	1.8	30.51	0.05	—	45	11.3
水 Water	¼ 杯 C. 60	—	60	0	0	0	0	—	—
薯餅吸油量 Cooking Oil Absorbed	4 大匙 T. 60	540	0	0	60	0	0	—	—
合 計 Total		2328	377.9	13.9	92.4	362.8	62.5	2018.8	208.1
一人份 Per Serving		388	63	2.3	15.4	60.5	10.4	336.5	34.7

材料：
芋頭(圖1)········180公克
西貢米(圖2)····· 50公克
糖····················¾杯
水····················15杯

① { 水·············· 4大匙
　　太白粉········ 2大匙

❶將芋頭切成指甲狀大小(約0.5×0.8公分)，備用。
❷將水7杯燒滾後，入芋頭片，以小火煮至爛(約15分鐘)備用。
❸將水8杯燒滾入西貢米，以小火煮至熟(約5分鐘)，撈出入芋頭中拌勻，續入糖溶化後，以①料勾芡即成。
■糖1杯約210公克。

INGREDIENTS:

180g (6⅓ oz)	Pared Taro (Illust. ①)
50g (1¾ oz)	Tapioca (Illust. ②)
¾ c.	Sugar
15 c.	Water
① { 4 T.	Water } mix
2 T.	Cornstarch }

❶ Chop taro (approx. 0.5×0.8 cm).
❷ Boil 7 c. water, add chopped taro and cook until soft (about 15 minutes). Set aside.
❸ Boil remaining 8 c. water, add tapioca and stir over low heat until transparent (about 15 minutes). Drain and set aside. Reheat pot of cooked taro; add drained tapioca and sugar. Stir until sugar dissolved; stir in mixture ① to thicken and serve.

項目 Item 材料 Material	份量·重量 Unit/Wt. (公克)(g)	熱量 Energy (卡)(Cal.)	水份 H₂O (公克)(g)	蛋白質 Prot. (公克)(g)	脂肪 Fat (公克)(g)	醣類 CHO (公克)(g)	鈉 Na (毫克)(mg)	鉀 K (毫克)(mg)	磷 P (毫克)(mg)
芋頭 Taro	180	201.6	121.14	5.58	0.36	45.36	9	927	108
西貢米 Tapioca	50	160	5.50	—	—	40	—	—	81.5
糖 Sugar	¾ 杯 C. 60	640	—	0	0	160	1.6	4	—
水 Water	10 杯 C. 2400	0	2400	0	0	0	—	—	—
太白粉 Cornstarch	2 大匙 T. 30	101.1	—	0.38	0.08	24	1.8	2.7	0
合計 Total	1103	1806.6	1806.6	6	0.4	269.4	12.4	933.7	189.5
一人份 Per Serving	184	301.1	301.1	1	0.07	44.9	2	155.6	31.6

南瓜塔 Pumpkin Tarts

材料：

外皮部份
瑪琪琳…………2大匙（30公克）
糖粉…………20公克
蛋…………⅓個
澄粉…⅔杯（90公克）
酸粉…………⅛小匙
香草片…………⅓片

內餡部份
南瓜（去皮）100公克
蛋…………⅓個
黑糖··3大匙（45公克）
澄粉…………1小匙
肉桂粉…………¼小匙
塩、豆寇粉各⅛小匙
丁香粉…………少許
鮮奶··3大匙（45公克）

外皮：
❶香草片壓碎與澄粉、酸粉拌勻，過篩後，備用。
❷將瑪琪琳放入鋼盆內，加入糖粉，以直型打蛋器拌勻，再加蛋及過篩後之❶料，以橡皮刮刀拌勻後，分成6等分，再放入已抹油的模型中，用手按成凹狀，即成外皮（圖1）。

內餡作法：
❶南瓜放入蒸鍋中蒸至爛（約20分鐘）拿出瀝乾，攪成泥備用。
❷所有材料拌勻，分成6等分裝入各個外皮中（圖2），以205℃（400°F）烤25分鐘，即成。
■一個蛋的可食部份約50公克。

INGREDIENTS:

Crust:
30g (1 oz)	Margarine
20g (⅔ oz)	Confectioner's Sugar
⅓	Egg
⅔ c. (90g/3 oz)	Wheat Starch
⅛ t.	Baking Power
⅓	Vanilla Tablet

Filling:
100g (3½ oz)	Pared Pumpkin
⅓	Egg
3 T. (45g/1⅗ oz)	Brown Sugar
1 t.	Wheat Starch
¼ t.	Cinnamon Powder
⅛ t. each	Nutmeg Powder, Salt
a dash	Ground Cloves
3 T. (45g/1⅗ oz)	Fresh Milk

Crust:
❶ Crush ⅓ vanilla tablet, mix with wheat starch and baking powder. Sift and set aside.
❷ In a metal mixing bowl, cream margarine and confectioner's sugar with rotary egg beater. Add ⅓ egg and dry ingredients from step ❶. Mix thoroughly until smooth (with rubber spatula), and divide pastry into 6 portions. Lightly grease 6 molds (tart pans or muffin cups) and fit pastry in. Press to leave space for filling (Illust. ①).

Filling:
❶ Steam pumpkin until soft (about 20 minutes). Remove and drain. Mash and set aside.
❷ Mix mashed pumpkin with rest of ingredients for filling. Divide into 6 portions. Fill each lined mold with a portion of the filling (Illust. ②); smooth out surface, and bake at 205°C (400°F) for 25 minutes.

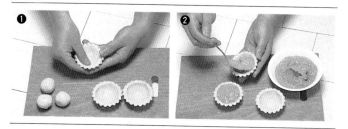

材料 Material	份量·重量 Unit/Wt. (公克)(g)	熱量 Energy (卡)(Cal.)	水份 H₂O (公克)(g)	蛋白質 Prot. (公克)(g)	脂肪 Fat (公克)(g)	糖類 CHO (公克)(g)	鈉 Na (毫克)(mg)	鉀 K (毫克)(mg)	磷 P (毫克)(mg)
瑪琪琳 Margarine	2 大匙T. 30	200	4.8	+	24	+	30	6	6
糖粉 Sugar	20	80	+	—	—	20	—	—	—
蛋 Egg	⅔個PC. 34	58.82	24.72	4.25	4.35	0.27	40.8	44.2	61.2
澄粉 Whole Wheat Flour	¾杯C. 95	320.45	—	1.19	0.24	76	5.7	8.6	0
酸粉 Baking Powder	⅛小匙t. 0.63	0	0	0	0	0	32.8	1	18
黑糖 Brown Sugar	45	141.3	6.75	0.86	0	35.73	13	154.4	8.1
南瓜 Pumpkin	100	2.4	90.8	0.9	0.3	5.5	2	228	26
鮮奶 Milk	3 大匙T. 45	30.6	39.51	1.35	1.62	2.16	22	68	41
塩 Salt	⅛小匙t. 0.63	0	0	0	0	0	163.8	0	0
合計 Total		834	166.6	8.6	30.5	139.7	310.1	510.2	160.3
一人份 Per Serving		139	27.8	1.4	5.1	23.3	51.7	85	26.7

材料：

瑪琪琳	⅜杯	葡萄乾	30粒
糖粉	¾杯	① 澄粉	1¼杯
雞蛋	½個	酸粉	1小匙
香草片	1片	細塩	⅛小匙
杏仁精	1大匙		

❶ 將瑪琪琳放入不銹鋼盆中，以直型打蛋器攪拌3分鐘，續入糖粉拌勻(約5分鐘)，①料用篩子篩過，香草片壓碎均勻備用。

❷ 蛋加入糖、油中，攪拌均勻後，續入①料、壓碎之香草片及杏仁精拌勻，即成"生料"。

❸ 用一只菊花口模型，裝入生料，以拇指擠花在烤盤上(共30個)，並放葡萄乾在上面裝飾，最後以190℃(380°F)烤8至10分鐘即成。

■ 1杯澄粉130公克
■ 瑪琪琳1杯225公克

INGREDIENTS:

⅜ c.		Margarine
¾ c.		Confectioner's Sugar
½		Egg
1		Vanilla Tablet
1 T.		Almond Extract
30		Raisins
①	1¼ c.	Wheat Starch
	1 t.	Baking Powder
	⅛ t.	Salt

❶ In a metal mixing bowl, beat margarine with a rotary egg beater for 3 minutes. Fold in confectioner's sugar and continue beating for 5 more minutes or until thoroughly mixed. Set aside. Sift dry ingredients ①, crush vanilla tablet and set aside.

❷ Add ½ egg to margarine/sugar mixture and blend well. Add sifted ①, crushed vanilla tablet and almond extract. Mix thoroughly and divide dough into 30 portions.

❸ Force dough through a cookie press, top with raisin and bake at 190°C (380°F) for 8 to 10 minutes.

項目 Item / 材料 Material	份量・重量 Unit/Wt. (g)	熱量 (卡) Energy (Cal.)	水份 (公克) H2O (g)	蛋白質 (公克) Prot. (g)	脂肪 (公克) Fat (g)	糖類 (公克) CHO (g)	鈉 (毫克) Na (mg)	鉀 (毫克) K (mg)	磷 (毫克) P (mg)
瑪琪琳 Margarine	⅜杯 C. 85	750.60	0	0	84.92	0	85	17	17
糖粉 Sugar	¾杯 C. 97.5	390	—	0	0	97.5	—	—	—
雞蛋 Egg	½個 PC. 25	43.25	23.18	3.13	3.2	0.2	30	32.5	45
香草片 Vanilla	1片 PC.								
澄粉 Whole Wheat Flour	1¼杯 C. 162	545.94	—	2.03	0.41	129.6	9.7	14.6	0
酸粉 Baking Powder	1小匙 t. 5	—	—	—	—	—	547.7	8.3	145
塩 Salt	⅛小匙 t. 0.63	—	0.04	—	—	—	244	0	0
杏仁精 Almond Ex.	1大匙 T. 15	—	15	—	—	—	—		
合計 Total		1730	38.2	5.2	88.5	227.3	916.4	72.4	207
一人份 Per Serving		288	6.4	0.9	14.8	37.9	152.7	12	34.5

椰 子 塔 Coconut Tarts

材料：

外皮部份
瑪琪琳	3大匙
糖粉	¼杯
蛋	½個
澄粉	1杯
酸粉	⅛小匙
香草片	½片

內餡部份
瑪琪琳	1大匙
糖粉	½杯
蛋	½個
奶水	1大匙
椰子粉	¾杯

外皮：
❶香草片壓碎與澄粉、酸粉拌勻，過篩後，備用。
❷將瑪琪琳放入鋼盆內，加入糖粉，以直型打蛋器拌勻，再加蛋及上述❶料，以橡皮刮刀拌勻後分成6等分，再放入已抹油的模型中，用手按成凹型，即爲外皮。
內餡作法：
❶瑪琪琳加入糖粉、蛋，以直型打蛋器調勻後，再加入奶水、椰子粉一齊攪拌至均勻，然後分成6等分，裝入各個外皮中，壓平整型後，以205℃ (400°F)烤25分鐘，即成。
■酸粉1小匙3公克

INGREDIENTS:
Crust:
3 T.	Margarine
¼ c.	Confectioner's Sugar
½	Egg
1 c.	Wheat Starch
⅛ t.	Baking Powder
½	Vanilla Tablet

Filling:
1 T.	Margarine
½ c.	Confectioner's Sugar
½	Egg
1 T.	Evaporated Milk
¾ c.	Shredded Coconut

Crust:
❶ Crush vanilla tablet, mix with wheat starch and baking powder. Sift and set aside.
❷ In a metal mixing bowl, blend margarine and confectioner's sugar thoroughly with rotary egg beater. Add ½ egg, sifted dry ingredients from step ❶ and mix until smooth. With a rubber spatula, divide pastry into 6 portions. Lightly grease 6 molds (fluted tart pans or muffin cups) and fit pastry in. Press to leave space for filling.
Filling:
❶ In a metal mixing bowl, blend margarine, confectioner's sugar and ½ egg thoroughly with rotary egg beater. Add evaporated milk and shredded coconut. Mix until smooth and divide into 6 portions. Fill each lined mold with a portion of the filling; smooth out surface, and bake at 205°C (400°F) for 25 minutes.

項目 Item / 材料 Material	份量・重量（公克）Unit/Wt (g)	熱量（卡）Energy (Cal.)	水份（公克）H₂O (g)	蛋白質（公克）Prot. (g)	脂肪（公克）Fat (g)	糖類（公克）CHO (g)	鈉（毫克）Na (mg)	鉀（毫克）K (mg)	磷（毫克）P (mg)
瑪琪琳 Margarine	4 大匙 T. 60	529.8	0	0	59.9	0	60	12	12
糖粉 Sugar	¾ 杯 C. 97.5	390	0	0	0	97.5	—	—	—
蛋 Egg	1 個 PC. 50	86.5	36.35	6.25	6.4	0.4	60	65	90
澄粉 Whole Wheat Flour	1 杯 C. 130	438.1	—	1.63	0.33	104	7.8	11.7	0
奶水 Evaporated Milk	1 大匙 T. 15	22.39	18	1.39	1.08	1.78	19	55	36.7
酸粉 Baking Powder	⅛ 小匙 t. 0.38	—	—	—	—	—	41.62	0.6	11
椰子粉 Shredded Coconut	¾ 杯 C. 58	202.5	—	2.25	20.7	5.4	—	309.3	96.7
香草片 Vanilla	½ 片 PC.	—	—	—	—	—	—	—	—
合計 Total		1669	54.4	11.5	88.4	209.1	188.4	453.6	246.4
一人份 Per Serving		278	9.1	1.9	14.7	34.9	31.4	75.6	41.1

材料：

瑪琪琳	150公克	酸粉	2½小匙
糖粉	1½杯	細塩	¼小匙
雞蛋	3個	香草片	2片
澄粉	2½杯	水	½杯

❶香草片壓碎與澄粉、酸粉、細塩拌勻、過篩，備用。
❷瑪琪琳以直型打蛋器攪拌一下，糖粉分三次加入拌勻後，再將蛋一個一個加入，最後加入已過篩之❶料攪拌均勻。
❸長型模型塗好瑪琪琳，倒入麵糊，以177℃ (350°F) 烤30分鐘左右，即成。
■如果飲食中限制蛋白質較嚴格時，可以清水代替雞蛋的份量。
■糖粉1杯130公克，酸粉1小匙3公克。

INGREDIENTS:

150g (5¼ oz)	Margarine
3	Eggs
2½ c.	Wheat Starch
1½ c.	Confectioner's Sugar
2½ t.	Baking Powder
¼ t.	Salt
a dash	Vanilla Extract
½ c.	Water

❶ Mix wheat starch, baking powder, and salt. Sift and set aside.
❷ Cream margarine with rotary egg beater, and gradually work in confectioner's sugar. Mix until smooth; beat in eggs one by one; add vanilla extract; and fold in sifted dry ingredients from step ❶. Beat vigorously.
❸ Pour batter into greased loaf pan and bake at 177°C (350°F) for approximately 30 minutes.
■ In cases where protein intake must be strictly restricted, water may be used in place of eggs.

項目 Item 材料 Material	份量・重量 (公克) Unit/Wt. (g)	熱量 (卡) Energy (Cal.)	水份 (公克) H₂O (g)	蛋白質 (公克) Prot. (g)	脂肪 (公克) Fat (g)	醣類 (公克) CHO (g)	鈉 (毫克) Na (mg)	鉀 (毫克) K (mg)	磷 (毫克) P (mg)
瑪琪琳 Margarine	150	1324.5	0	0	149.85	0	150	30	30
糖粉 Sugar	1½ 杯 C. 195	780	2.73	0	0	195	—	—	—
蛋 Egg	3 個 PC. 150	259.5	109.05	18.75	19.20	1.2	180	195	270
澄粉 Whole Wheat Flour	2½ 杯 C. 325	1095.3	—	4.06	0.81	260	19.5	29.3	0
酸粉 Baking Powder	2½ 小匙 t. 7.5	—	—	—	—	—	821.5	12.5	217.5
細塩 Salt	¼ 小匙 t. 1.25	—	0.09	—	—	—	487.5	0.05	—
香草片 Vanilla	2 片 PC.	—	—	—	—	—	—	—	—
水 Water	½ 杯 C. 120	0	120	0	0	0	0	0	0
合計 Total		3459	111.9	22.8	169.9	456.2	1658.5	266.9	517.50
一人份 Per Serving		345.9	11.2	2.3	16.9	45.6	165.9	26.7	51.8

齒頰生香的美味

濃稠的醬汁，獨特的風味 ———

味全烤肉醬，烤出餐桌上動人的美味，

品賞似的一口，嗯——齒頰生香……

味全烤肉醬，可沾、燒、煎、烤，用

途多，風味好。

味全烤肉醬
兩種口味・辣／不辣

味全
wei chuan

烤肉醬
BAR-B-Q SAUCE

辣味

味全罐頭上口系列、豬肉鬆，質鮮味美——

愈吃愈上口！

上口系列

味全
豬肉鬆

味全
上口脆瓜

味全
上口小菜心

味全
上口花生麵筋

味全
香菇麵筋

創造和樂的社會

我們的理想

　　本著"取之於社會，用之於社會"的理想，味全文化教育基金會自民國68年成立以來，即不斷積極於培育專門人才，促進家庭和諧，致力國際交流，創造安和社會，成果卓著，廣受社會大眾的肯定與支持。

　　以行動實踐服務社會的熱誠，每年舉辦兒童冬夏令營、幸福家庭系列專題講座、婦女二度就業服務、金廚獎烹飪比賽、金雕獎雕塑比賽、紅毯之旅……等社會公益活動。

味全文化教育基金會

住址：台北市松江路125號5樓
電話：5063564・5065001・5084331

爲生活增添趣味

使家庭更幸福美滿

　　美好的日子是需要去創造的，味全家政班以"增進生活情趣，提昇精神層次"的理念，多年來，除致力於各種家政技藝的傳承外，更隨社會的需求，廣開多樣性的學習課程，期使每個家庭成員在工作忙碌之餘，生活得多姿多釆。

- ●烹飪班：中國菜、西餐、中點、西點、餐盤裝飾等……。
- ●插花班：西洋花、池坊流、小原流。
- ●美姿班：瑜伽、韻律。
- ●語文班：英語、日語。
- ●兒童才藝班：
  繪畫、心算、書法、英語、作文、韻律、鋼琴、課後輔導等。

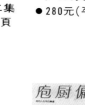

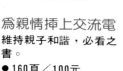